THE ME I SEE

THE ME I SEE

A CHRISTIAN APPROACH TO SELF-ESTEEM

Though this book is designed for group study, it is also intended for your personal enjoyment and spiritual growth. A leader's guide is available from your local bookstore or from your publisher.

Beacon Hill Press of Kansas City
Kansas City, Mo.

Editor
Everett Leadingham

Editorial Assistant
Bryan Merrill

Editorial Committee
Randy Cloud
Everett Leadingham
Thomas Mayse
Bryan Merrill
Stephen M. Miller
Gene Van Note
Carl Pierce

Copyright 1994
by Beacon Hill Press of Kansas City

ISBN 083-411-5204
Printed in the United States of America

Bible Credits

Unless otherwise indicated, all Scripture quotations are taken from the *Holy Bible, New International Version*® (NIV®). Copyright © 1973, 1978, 1984 by International Bible Society. Used by permission of Zondervan Publishing House. All rights reserved.

Permission to quote from the following Scripture version is acknowledged with appreciation:

New American Standard Bible (NASB), © 1960, 1962, 1963, 1968, 1971, 1972, 1973, 1975, 1977 by The Lockman Foundation.

New Revised Standard Version (NRSV), copyright 1989 by the Division of Christian Education of the National Council of Churches of Christ in the USA. All rights reserved.

The King James Version (KJV).

10   9   8   7   6   5   4   3   2   1

Contents

▼▼▼
A Quick Look Ahead

- In this pop-psychology age, almost everyone is aware of the need for a healthy perception of self—parents, teachers, managers, and lawyers.

- Self-esteem is self-perception—how we view and value that internal person we believe ourselves to be. That understanding is not always based on reality. It is our impression of ourselves that has a dominating influence in forming attitudes about the self.

- What we view as successful is affected by our history, our contemporary culture, and our values. Standards of success that are grounded in reality help us measure our worth. The problem lies in standards that are unreasonable and unreachable. For the one whose self-esteem is centered in financial success, how much money is enough? For the perfectionist, how clean does the house have to be before it is acceptable for guests?

- All of life's experiences form our sense of self-worth. But finding our ultimate worth in Christ helps us interpret all of those experiences with a clearer perspective of what is really valuable.

1

Sources of Self-Esteem

by Ed Robinson

I'VE NOTICED them often, in many crowded rooms:

● Some stand apart from the crowd, disappearing into the woodwork. Others are right in the middle, pressing the limits of civility with boisterous behavior.

● Some speak so softly their words are barely audible. Others fill the room with a barrage of decibels matching a roaring engine.

● Some refuse to enter a discussion that requires some opinion or judgment, appealing to the belief they never have a good idea. Others dominate the discussion, positive that their perspective not only is right but is the only one.

● Some turn to stone when touched by another person. Others crave physical contact, sometimes hanging on the arm of a friend, parent, or even casual acquaintance.

Who are these people? What could they possibly have in common? Each may have a low self-esteem.

"Self-esteem" is not a new word in the modern vocabulary. The idea has been around for a long time. Previously, only psychologists or teachers used it much. In recent years "self-image," "self-worth," or "self-actualization" (it comes in a variety of names) has become a part of everyday conversation.

In this pop-psychology age, almost everyone is aware of the need for a healthy perception of self. Parents are warned to treat their children carefully so as not to bruise their fragile egos. Teachers are encouraged to treat their students in ways that bolster their confidence. Managers are taught that belittling their employees will cut down on productivity and profit. Workers who feel better about themselves and the company will work harder, longer, and more efficiently than those who do not feel appreciated. The value of self-esteem has infiltrated the legal system. Even lawyers have appealed to the influence of low self-esteem on people to divert blame or explain illegal actions. The concept of self-esteem is a powerful force in today's society.

Self-esteem: A Matter of Perspective

Basically, self-esteem is self-perception—how we view and value that internal person we believe ourselves to be. That understanding is not always based on reality. It is our impression of ourselves that has a dominating influence in forming attitudes about the self.

I know some teenage girls who think they are overweight, when, in fact, they are skinny compared to the average population. But if their perception tells them they are "fat," they believe it. In a mild form, such a perception leads to unnecessary dieting. In severe forms, it may result in serious eating disorders like anorexia nervosa.

Sources of self-esteem can be any experience, observation, or conversation that influences self-perceptions. These influences have both a positive and negative effect. Imagine that each person has a subconscious self-esteem ledger sheet with a positive (+) and a negative (-) column. All of the various experiences of life are recorded in one of the two columns. They contribute to either a positive or a negative attitude toward self.

The positive column might include:

+ encouraging words from parents
+ an award received at school
+ a project finished on schedule
+ a favorable job review or
+ acceptance by a special friend

The negative column might include:

- belittling comments from a parent
- failing the "chin-ups" portion of the third grade physical fitness test
- a cruel comment about out-of-style clothes in junior high school
- a rejection when not invited to the most important high school party of the year or
- being passed over for a management position

I remember one experience that was recorded in my negative column. It happened over 30 years ago, but I remember it as if it were yesterday. I have had a robust physique since I was 8 years old. At age 12, I was warming up before a basketball game. I was already self-conscious that my basketball jersey fit tightly. One of the opposing players walked by and made a loud comment that suggested I was a girl. I was devastated. I wanted to disappear into the floor. To this day, I am still conscious about how shirts and sweaters fit when I try on clothes. I tell myself in my maturity I have gotten over that caustic remark. But the truth is, that single, 30-year-old incident still shapes my self-perception.

All of the experiences or observations that form our self-esteem need not be dramatic. In fact, most of them are filed somewhere—not actively remembered but still influential.

So what determines whether we have a positive or a negative self-image? If the positive ledger is stronger than the negative one, we can function adequately in life with a sense of confidence and fulfillment. If the negative ledger is dominant, our attitudes and actions will reflect our negative image. Our perception of ourselves depends largely on how we have processed the collection of life's experiences, observations, and conversations. Remember, it isn't the reality that determines our self-worth; it's our *perception* of those formative events.

Common Sources of Self-Esteem

While all personal experiences form our self-perceptions, some factors seem to be more critical than others. The relationship with our parents is a basic source of self-esteem. Our perception of self begins in the earliest stages of life. Many prominent psychologists point to the development of a child's ability to trust others as foundational. Trusting a parent or other caregiver for warmth, food, safety, and security allows a person in later stages of life to trust a friend, business associate, or spouse. When babies do not experience the faithful commitment and acceptance in life's basic needs, they often have lifelong difficulty committing themselves to loving relationships with others. They fear rejection or loss, so they never take significant risks. Or conversely, they may try so hard to meet their intense need to be loved and accepted, they inappropriately throw themselves on others, without providing a solid framework for the relationship.

Healthy relationships require significant commitment. Such commitment requires trust. Trust requires a healthy dose of self-esteem, beginning in childhood. As we progress through life, other critical issues—independence, competence, identity, and social contribution—are dependent on our self-image. Self-esteem is a lifelong issue, framed significantly on the foundation of our self-perceptions in childhood.

Our standards of success and significance also serve as a source of self-esteem. Most of us feel good about ourselves when we can live up to our standards. An objective achieved, a challenge conquered, a degree earned, an obstacle overcome—all contribute to a healthy self-awareness. We only have to experience the joy of a child who has just completed a somersault and rises to exclaim, "Look what I did, all by myself!" to understand the power of living up to a standard in shaping self-esteem.

What we view as successful is affected by our history, our contemporary culture, and our values. Standards of success that are grounded in reality are invaluable in helping us measure our worth. The problem lies in standards that are unreasonable. When we establish goals that are unreachable, we set ourselves up for a huge entry into the negative column of the self-esteem ledger.

For the one whose self-esteem is centered in financial success, how much money is enough? For the perfectionist, how clean does the house have to be before it is acceptable for guests? For those who can't keep a significant relationship, how lovable must they become to accept the love of another? For those who have difficulty accepting God's gracious offer of salvation, how righteous must they become before God would want a personal relationship with them? In each of these instances, the standard is either out of balance or simply untrue. Such standards create false guilt, negative attitudes, and sometimes depression.

Our daily interaction with significant persons in our lives results from and shapes self-esteem. Trying to determine if these experiences form our self-esteem or if our self-esteem determines the quality of our associations is a bit like trying to solve the proverbial dilemma—which came first, the chicken or the egg?

When our interpersonal relationships are character-ized by trust, commitment, forgiveness, and encourage-ment, our self-worth flourishes. We can trust more readily, commit more deeply, and encourage more naturally. Our self-image is strengthened as a result of our relationships. And our relationships are strengthened as our self-image flourishes.

The reverse is also true. When our interpersonal rela-tions are characterized by competition, skepticism, and mistrust, our self-esteem suffers. As our self-image goes down, our attitudes about ourselves and others become distorted and negative, affecting the quality of our rela-tionships. This vicious cycle often continues until we find ourselves living in little boxes of isolation from others, even while working in the same office, attending the same church, or living in the same house.

Daily interactions shape our attitudes. Those attitudes shape our sense of self-worth. Self-worth reinforces our ap-proach to our daily interactions. All three dimensions in-teract and reinforce themselves—to either positive or nega-tive ends.

The Ultimate Source of Self-Esteem

There is still a more important ingredient that devel-ops our image of self.

To think that our self-esteem depends on influences that are, to a large degree, beyond our control can be rather discouraging. There are too many possibilities in the self-esteem equation for us to figure out. It might seem to some like purely chance—some people are lucky to have more good experiences, while others have more negative ones.

The good news is there are ultimate and constant foundations for everyone. The first is as old as creation— we are all created by God. That very fact gives us inherent value. Listen to some of the ways God's own revelation speaks about us:

> Then God said, "Let us make man in our image, in our likeness. . . ." So God created man in his own image, in the image of God he created him; male and female he created them. . . . God saw all that he had made, and it was very good *(Gen. 1:26-27, 31).*

> When I consider your heavens, the work of your fingers, the moon and the stars, which you have set in place, what is man that you are mindful of him, the son of man that you care for him? You made him a little lower than the heavenly beings and crowned him with glory and honor *(Ps. 8:3-5).*

> For you created my inmost being; you knit me together in my mother's womb. I praise you because I am fearfully and wonderfully made; your works are wonderful, I know that full well *(Ps. 139:13-14).*

The fact that we are a significant part of creation is an unchanging reality. In the shifting sands of life's experiences, God's view of us is constant.

We live in a world where most everything must be earned. We hear early in our lives that we must earn trust and respect. We must make our own way in the world, be self-sufficient. We even pride ourselves in our independence.

Unfortunately, we transpose the self-sufficient, earn-our-own-way attitude into the deepest and most significant relationship of life—our relationship with God. We struggle to make ourselves worthy of that relationship. We set a standard of righteousness to which we must attain so that God will ascribe value to us. That effort is futile. We can never make ourselves worthy enough. When we try, we find ourselves coming up short. So we try harder the next time, and the next, and the next. . . . As this cycle of defeat spirals downward, our self-image hits bottom—with despair.

Our self-esteem, in this cycle of defeat, is not based on reality. We cannot make ourselves worthy of God. God is the only one who can make us worthy. We cannot earn the right to be in relationship with Him. He is the only one who can initiate that relationship. It is grace—unearned favor—that gives us ultimate value. God considered us to be of such unlimited value that He sacrificed the One He loves most so that we might be accepted by Him forever (John 3:16). That grace never changes. In the person of Jesus Christ, crucified and resurrected, we find ultimate value, the ideal of self-esteem.

As we grow in grace and learn to commit ourselves to the holiness of God, we begin to view ourselves and those around us differently. As Paul wrote to the Corinthians:

So from now on we regard no one from a worldly point of view. Though we once regarded Christ in this way, we do so no longer. Therefore, if anyone is in Christ, he is a new creation; the old has gone, the new has come! *(2 Cor. 5:16-17).*

We have a new way of looking at reality. But what about all the other entries on the self-esteem ledger, some of them many years old? The two constant sources of value—our worth in the created order and God's grace given through Christ—should heavily influence how we perceive life's past, present, and future experiences. Some will still be entered in the negative column, but many more will find their way into the positive since we have a better perception of reality. Being able to forgive can move some entries from one side to another. Setting realistic goals for our lives can transfer some experiences from one side of the ledger to another. Keeping an eternal perspective on some daily issues of life can help us to more adequately cope and accurately perceive how they affect our worth.

I have a friend at church who felt like she had little to offer. She had just gone through a divorce. Many people in the congregation didn't understand the circumstances and criticized her. She stopped serving. She came late to services and left early so that she wouldn't have to speak to people. Her self-esteem was very low. Through a Bible study, my friend began to rediscover the grace of God and the reality of her worth to Him and to the church.

I can still remember the evening she asked us to pray for her because she had been asked to give her testimony in the evening service. She said, "I don't know if I can do this."

We said, "God believes in you, and so do we. You can do it!" I watched as God rebuilt her life. She shared her testimony about the grace of God at work within her. She started serving again. She started believing in herself because God, and a group of His people, believed in her.

All of life's experiences form our sense of self-worth. But finding our ultimate worth in Christ helps us interpret all of those experiences with a clearer perspective of what is really valuable. Since self-esteem is largely a matter of self-perception, any self-esteem based primarily on sources other than the ultimate source is distorted.

Self-esteem: A Final Word

For Christians, self-esteem is never the final word. The essential difference between much of the current psychological search for self-actualization and the Christian perspective of self-worth is in the outcome. Generally, only the individual's own personality is the focus of psychological self-actualization—"be all *you* can be," "find the real *you*," "get in touch with *your* inner self," and so forth. An individual focus for its own sake is never sufficient for the Christian. Our focus is always beyond the self. We find our true self in our relationship with God and others. It is only by giving ourselves away that we actually find what it means to be whole.

Background Scripture: Gen. 1:26-31; Pss. 8:3-5; 139:13-16; John 3:16; 2 Cor. 5:16-17

Ed Robinson is a professor of religious education at Nazarene Theological Seminary in Kansas City.

▼▼▼

A Quick Look Ahead

- Is anyone ever "just" anything—housewife, truck driver, supermarket cashier, baby-sitter, factory worker, sales-clerk, or church secretary? How we view ourselves and how we view others determines the nature of our relation-ships.

- If we want to know what people are really like, we can observe the way they treat people considered inferior.

- Every job within the Body of Christ is important. If we could see with God's eyes, we'd be much less impressed with certain individuals and greatly humbled by others. Mrs. Surly viewed herself as an underpaid, overworked cafeteria worker. Mr. Archibald saw himself as a worth-while person who made an honest living for his family working in a school cafeteria.

- Job titles say nothing about a person's value or potential contribution to the Body of Christ. If Jesus had carried a union card, His occupation would have been listed as "carpenter." Would the carpenter who built our garage be welcome at our dinner table?

2

What Do I Do for a Living? Oh, I'm Just a . . .

by Leola Floren Gee

BETTY IS the white-haired mother of three grown sons. Now in her 60s, her unpaid occupations for many years have been teaching women's Bible studies and keeping house for her family.

Ask Betty about her accomplishments, and she'll list the attributes of her extraordinary grandchildren. Ask about her home, and she'll describe the neat-as-a-pin condominium in suburban Detroit to which she and her husband retired. Ask about her status in life, and the answer will be no less direct. "I'm the daughter of a King," she'll say, dark eyes sparkling. She would never say, "I'm just a housewife."

Is anyone ever "just" anything—housewife, truck driver, supermarket cashier, baby-sitter, factory worker, salesclerk, or church secretary?

How we view ourselves and how we view others determines the nature of our relationships. When we look at another person and see "just" someone doing his or her job, we aren't as inclined to give the respect that is necessary to establish a relationship.

We can take the hint from Betty and learn to view ourselves and others as royalty. What a difference that will make in our relationships wherever we are.

Lifestyles of the Not-So-Famous and Nearly Broke

We live in a status-conscious society, in which we are judged by our wealth and professional titles. Turn on the television. It's easy to find a show devoted to celebrity watching. In one well-known show, "Lifestyles of the Rich and Famous," the host jets around the world to profile entertainers and entrepreneurs who have gathered expensive homes, cars, clothes, private yachts, and art collections.

My husband and I have an extensive art collection, but most of it is attached to the refrigerator with magnets. Few of us have summer homes on Cape Cod or bank accounts in Switzerland, so it's tempting to get caught up in the glitzy glamour of the lives of those who do.

As a journalist, I've had the opportunity to observe several celebrities up close. I find the most revealing performances occur off-camera.

On one occasion, I spent two days with a violin prodigy in his early 20s who had received lots of national publicity. He was talented. On "The Tonight Show" he had been completely charming. Yet, as I watched him on the racquetball court exercising before a rehearsal, I saw a poor loser with an uncontrollable temper.

Throughout both days I watched him treat underlings with indifference or contempt. To him everyone, including the hotel staff and his accompanist, was a subordinate. Though the music that poured from his violin at the concert was technically outstanding, it rang hollow to me because of his arrogance.

His accompanist was another story. A kind, humble gentleman, he understood that he needed to remain in the shadows so that the star could shine. While a photographer and I watched him practice, he was oblivious to beads of sweat that rolled off the tip of his nose. He was delighted to play for us—at no charge. Sharing the loveliness of the music with an appreciative audience was his pleasure.

Which of the two men used his abilities the way God intended? The former viewed his gift as a stepping-stone to fame, financial success, and high status. The latter used his gift to feed his own soul and the souls of strangers listening to him practice in an otherwise-deserted room. The pianist is a greater musician than the violinist, I think.

If we want to know what people are really like, we can observe the way they treat people considered inferior. I've noticed that if I ask a successful businessperson about life philosophy when the tape recorder is running, he or she will speak eloquently regarding love for humanity and concern for the betterment of society. But if I want to look into the heart, I listen to the manner in which he or she speaks to a secretary after the tape recorder is put away. Or I watch the treatment of a waiter in a restaurant when service is slow.

If we follow Christ's example, we will view every individual as a person created in God's image, worthy of our attention and respect. The lady behind the counter at the dry cleaner's is made in God's image. So is the bank teller. Even the young person who slopped mayonnaise on our hamburger when we asked for ketchup.

A Cafeteria Worker Serves Up Respect

It's one matter to take shots at celebrities whose lives are remote from ours. But status can also be an issue close to home. In our workplaces and churches, pecking orders develop that determine which individuals are most valued.

For instance, in church is it more prestigious to serve on the board or to work in the nursery? Is the senior pastor seen as more significant than the youth pastor? Is the soloist valued more highly than the choir member who is faithful in attendance and enjoys singing, though she is sometimes off-key?

Every job within the Body of Christ is important. In his comparison of spiritual gifts to the human body, Paul says, "The eye cannot say to the hand, 'I don't need you!' And the head cannot say to the feet, 'I don't need you!' On the contrary, those parts of the body that seem to be weaker are indispensable, and the parts that we think are less honorable we treat with special honor" (1 Cor. 12:21-23). If we could see with God's eyes, we'd be much less impressed with certain individuals and greatly humbled by others.

When I was in elementary school, a tall, slender man named Mr. Archibald* stood beside the garbage cans in the cafeteria. He cleared our trays and chided us good-naturedly if we dared to eat our dessert without first disposing of our green beans. Mr. Archibald was actually a janitor, but he considered himself a guardian of children. He performed his duties with humor and affection.

Twenty years later, I worked in an office building with a cafeteria similar to the one in elementary school. A woman I call Mrs. Surly* held a job similar to Mr. Archibald's. Mrs. Surly, however, let it be known that she resented every minute she had to spend working in a menial job, taking orders from supervisors, and mopping up after clumsy and obnoxious customers.

Who had the worst job? Mr. Archibald had to deal with noisy kids who rarely said thank you, frequently spilled their milk, and occasionally gagged after dumping mustard on their sloppy joes. He might not have enjoyed the actual work any more than Mrs. Surly did, yet he usually had a smile on his face.

The major difference between them, I suspect, is this: Mrs. Surly viewed herself as an underpaid, overworked cafeteria worker. Mr. Archibald saw himself as a worthwhile person who made an honest living for his family working in a school cafeteria.

It was the person's self-view, not the job title, that made the difference.

Would Jesus Have Qualified for a Major Credit Card?

Intellectually, we may know that a person's worth is not related to what he or she does for a living. But do we believe it? If we received two dinner invitations for the same evening, one from the mayor and the other from the man who repairs the mayor's car, how would we decide which to accept?

Look at the people who were involved in the life of Christ. Some unknown person built the manger in which He lay in Bethlehem. Someone made the sandals He wore as He traveled the countryside. Some nameless mother packed a little boy's lunch with five loaves and two fishes. Some kitchen worker washed the plates and cups following the Last Supper. An unidentified weaver wove the robe over which soldiers gambled at the Crucifixion.

None of these individuals is identified in Scripture. Each did his or her job anonymously, without acknowledgment or fanfare. Yet, each was involved in biblical history.

Most of us may perform several roles within our lifetime, but only God knows which will be of greatest value in eternity. David was both a shepherd and a king. In my view, his most poignant psalms grew out of the shepherding experience. Joseph was both a slave and a high-ranking government official, but his slave status illustrates God's redemptive work in his life. When Paul wasn't going about the business of evangelizing a continent, he made tents. When Lydia wasn't opening her home to the Early Church, she was selling dry goods. In light of these biblical occupations, how can we continue to evaluate the people we meet according to how they make their living?

A job title says nothing about a person's value or potential contribution to the Body of Christ. If Jesus had carried a union card, His occupation would have been listed as "carpenter." Would that give Him enough status to qualify for a major credit card? Probably not. But would the carpenter who built our garage be welcome at our dinner table, either?

Peel Potatoes to the Glory of God

Sometimes I think we spend too much time and energy trying to direct our children into the "right" professions, while neglecting a more important aspect of their education. It's not how they make an honest living that matters, but whether they do it for God's glory.

That truth is clearly presented in the award-winning film *Chariots of Fire*. It deals with the true story of missionary Eric Liddell's participation in the 1924 Olympics. Liddell, a Scotsman, was a gifted runner whose family devoted themselves to missionary work. Early in the film, he was struggling. He had felt that perhaps he should focus on becoming a missionary immediately rather than running. But he really wanted to try to win a spot on the Olympic team. He didn't know which was the more important work in God's estimation. When he learned the Olympic committee would require him to race on Sunday, he thought he should withdraw rather than compromise his conviction not to run on the Lord's Day.

Perplexed, he received wise advice from an older friend. "Eric, you can praise the Lord by peeling a spud. Don't compromise. Run in God's name, and let the world stand back in wonder."

Liddell did win Olympic gold, and without compromising his conviction not to run on a Sunday. And he went on to become a missionary. During World War II, he died in an internment camp in occupied China. Yet, this missionary's testimony is still known around the world.

For a brief time in his life, Eric Liddell's assignment—and his joy—was to run races. The remainder of his life he devoted to work in China. Both were used for God's glory.

Are we running for Olympic gold, preparing for the mission field, or peeling potatoes to feed our family? Whatever we do, we can do it for God's glory. We can take our current responsibility and plug it into the advice given to Eric Liddell:

"Be a secretary in God's name, and let the world stand back in wonder."

"Be a construction worker in God's name, and let the world stand back in wonder."

"Be a nursing home attendant in God's name, and let the world stand back in wonder."

"Be a janitor in God's name, and let the world stand back in wonder."

"Be a plumber in God's name, and let the world stand back in wonder."

"Be a Sunday School teacher in God's name, and let the world stand back in wonder."

"Be a homemaker in God's name, and let the world stand back in wonder."

"Be the pastor of a small church in God's name, and let the world stand back in wonder."

Any job done for God's glory is a job well done. Likewise, any job done only for its high status amounts to no more than a heap of ashes.

*Name has been changed.

Background Scripture: Genesis 39—41; Matt. 25:14-30; Acts 18:1-4; 1 Cor. 3:6-9

Leola Floren Gee is a freelance journalist in suburban Detroit.

▼▼▼
A Quick Look Ahead

- Mel had hoped for an apology. He had hoped for at least some attempt on his father's part to respond. He had hoped his father would say, "I love you," or at least, "I forgive you." Most of all, perhaps, he had hoped his father would say, "Please forgive me."

- Forgiveness and reconciliation are not the same thing. Forgiveness is something we can do all by ourselves, something we can make happen by our own decision. Reconciliation, however, requires the participation of another person.

- Sometimes efforts at reconciliation are not advisable. In cases of physical, sexual, or other kinds of abuse, it may not be safe to reconcile with the people who have wronged us. Sometimes reconciliation is not possible because the other person is no longer living.

- We can be at peace even when reconciliation isn't possible. We can survive emotional injury—not only survive but flourish as well. No matter how deep the wound, no matter how bitter the pain, once we forgive, we are no longer victims or mere survivors.

3

You Can Forgive Without Reconciling

by David Stoop and James Masteller

[Editor's note: The processes described in this chapter reflect practical methods of Christian counselors. The underlying assumption is that we are never alone in these kinds of circumstances. The Holy Spirit is always at work in every situation of a Christian's life. The Holy Spirit is effective where our human efforts fail.]

AS A CHILD, Mel* remembered two things about his father. First, he remembered that his father was almost silent—always distant—around him. When he did speak, he seemed only to complain that Mel had done something wrong. Second, Mel remembered that his father drank heavily. Sometimes when he drank, he would laugh and tell funny stories. Other times he became abusive and hit Mel. Mel never knew which to expect.

Years later, after he had grown up and left home, Mel felt he needed to be free from the harsh memories of life with his father. After an intense struggle, he was able to work through the process of forgiveness and release his father from the emotional IOU he had held against him. It was a great day when Mel could finally say, "I've forgiven him."

He then decided to take what seemed like the next logical step—to reconcile with his father. Knowing that he had released himself from the grip of his past was wonderful, but Mel wanted to go further. He wanted to patch things up with his dad and restore their relationship. Although he now lived almost 1,000 miles away from his father, he made a special trip just to spend time with him. "Dad," he said, "could we talk?"

Without saying a word, Mel's father sat down in his favorite chair. Mel pulled up another chair and sat down facing his dad. For nearly 30 minutes, Mel told his dad about the pent-up anger and hurt he had grown up with. He never accused, and he carefully avoided saying anything condemnatory about his father's actions. He spoke only of himself, reporting simply and objectively what he had experienced, and how he now wanted to make things right.

At the end he leaned forward and took his father's hand. "Dad," he said, "I've put aside all my anger and hurt. I hope you'll forgive me for the many ways I've failed you. I've always wanted to be a good son, to make you proud of me. That's what I want now—just for us to be a real father and son."

Mel's father had listened the entire time without saying a word or expressing any emotion. As Mel finished, his father pulled himself up from his chair, looked down at Mel, nodded his head slightly, and said, "Well . . ." Then he turned, walked down the hall to his bedroom and quietly closed the door. He did not come out that night, or even the next day before Mel left.

Several months later, Mel's father suffered a stroke. He

died two hours before Mel reached him.

In reviewing his attempt at reconciliation, Mel spoke of his confusion. When he left his father's house that day, Mel still had no idea how his father felt about what he had said, about what had happened between them, about him—about anything. His dad never gave him the slightest response.

"Why did he act like that?" Mel said. "What did I do wrong?"

"Let's try a different question," I suggested. "What did you *expect* to happen when you talked to him?"

"Expect?" Mel said. He shrugged his shoulders. "I don't know what I expected. Nothing, I guess."

"Really?" I replied. "If you didn't have any expectations, then how could you have been disappointed?"

Mel pondered that for a moment, then began to speak. The words tumbled out. He had hoped for an apology. He had hoped for at least some attempt on his father's part to respond. He had hoped his father would say, "I love you," or at least, "I forgive you." Most of all, perhaps, he had hoped his father would say, "Please forgive me."

"And now he's gone," Mel said with great sadness. He had *forgiven* his father. But he had not been able to *reconcile* with him. It was one of those sad facts of life that so many of us must face. Mel struggled for a long time over what he considered to be his own failure. Surely he could have made the reconciliation happen if he had just said the right things or said them the right way, or . . .

"The only failure," I finally told Mel, "is that you lumped together two things that are really separate. Forgiveness and reconciliation are not the same thing."

Forgiveness is something we can do all by ourselves, something we can make happen by our own decision. Reconciliation, however, requires the participation of another person. We cannot make it happen, no matter how hard we try.

Forgiveness and reconciliation are two separate and distinct processes. We *can* have one without the other. Working through the process of forgiveness is essential to our personal well-being and should always be pursued. Reconciliation is immensely valuable to us and should be pursued whenever possible—but it isn't always possible.

Mel was stuck on this point. He did not consider his forgiveness of his father to be complete because he and his father had not reconciled. They had not established a relationship of mutual love, or even mutual respect. He was confusing the two processes.

I pointed out to Mel that as long as he continued to hold this view, his father could continue to hold him hostage, even in the grave. What Mel needed to see was that forgiveness and reconciliation were separate things— that he *had* forgiven his father, fully and completely, even though they had not reconciled.

Mel's situation is not unusual. I frequently find myself listening to persons describe their inner struggle to forgive someone—especially someone close to them—and then tell of their frustration over the way their relationship is now continuing. "Now what?" they ask. "Now that I've forgiven them, why can't we get along?" In effect, they are assuming that the other person, by refusing to be reconciled, can "undo" their forgiveness. But that is not the way it works.

"I just want you to see that you really have forgiven them," I usually say. "You have done what you needed to do, what you *could* do. You have canceled the debt and freed yourself from the obstacles that held you back from inner peace. I know you're not reconciled with them. But you *have* forgiven them. Nothing can change that."

"But I still can't even *talk* to them," one woman, named Jill*, objected. Her parents and two sisters had turned against her years before, when she had gotten heavily involved in drugs. Since then, Jill had changed. She stopped taking drugs and finished school. Now she held a responsible job in an advertising firm and had been married for three years. "I mean, they won't *let* me talk to them," she continued. "When I call, they hang up as soon as they recognize my voice. All my letters come back marked, 'Return to Sender.' I don't know what to do."

"Have you forgiven any bad feelings you held against them?" I asked her.

"Well, yes, but . . ."

"Then you've done all *you* can do," I said. "Forgiving them is your job. It's under your control. But not reconciling—for that you need their cooperation. There's nothing more you can do. But that doesn't mean you haven't forgiven them. You have."

Jill understood. She continues to hope—as I do—that one day her family will relent, and the door to reconciliation will open up. In the meantime, she can continue to work through the process of forgiveness whenever bitterness rises up and can grieve over a family that isn't there—at least not for her.

It Takes Two

Reconciliation is a two-way street. It requires two people who are at least somewhat tracking with each other. It can occur only when both parties to a relationship want it to happen, when both have accepted their own responsibility for what went wrong, have sorted out their emotions, and have worked through the processes of both repentance and forgiveness. Stated simply: "You work through your side of it and ask for my forgiveness; I work through my

side of it and ask for your forgiveness. Then we can be reconciled."

In the well-known story of the prodigal son, a young
man takes his inheritance, leaves his family, and wastes all
his money in a faraway city. Broke and hungry, he makes
the difficult decision to go back home and seek reconciliation with his family. In heartrending terms, he begs his father to take him back: "Father, I have sinned against heav-
en and against you. I am no longer worthy to be called
your son; make me like one of your hired men" (Luke
15:18-19).

Clearly, the young man has had a change of heart. He
has clearly dealt with whatever grievances he once held
against his father—those things that prompted him to run
away in the first place. He has canceled whatever emotional debt he once held against his father and has come to him
repentant, seeking to be reconciled.

How does the father respond? He, too, appears to
have released his son from whatever grudge he may have
held. "But while he was still a long way off, his father saw
him and was filled with compassion for him; he ran to his
son, threw his arms around him and kissed him" (Luke
15:20). What a classic picture of repentance, forgiveness,
and reconciliation!

But then we meet a third character—the older brother.

Meanwhile, the older son was in the field. When
he came near the house, he heard music and dancing.
So he called one of the servants and asked him what
was going on. "Your brother has come," he replied,
"and your father has killed the fattened calf because
he has him back safe and sound."

The older brother became angry and refused to go
in. So his father went out and pleaded with him. But
he answered his father, "Look! All these years I've

been slaving for you and never disobeyed your orders. Yet you never gave me even a young goat so I
could celebrate with my friends. But when this son of
yours who has squandered your property with prosti-
tutes comes home, you kill the fattened calf for him!"
(Luke 15:25-30).

The older brother, in contrast to his father, offers us a
picture of reconciliation spurned. Clearly, he still bears
great resentment toward his younger brother for his reck-
less behavior. He also seems to be bitter toward his father
for welcoming the younger brother back. As the story un-
folds, we see the father attempting to be reconciled to his el-
dest son, trying to explain his actions in forgiving the
younger brother. As far as we know, the older brother was
unwilling to be reconciled to either his brother or his father.

Reconciliation is a two-way street. In this case forgiveness flowed in only one direction, and reconciliation was
not possible. The father and the younger brother were free
from the prison of their bitterness and resentment; the older brother was still held.

When It Isn't Possible

I believe in the importance of reconciliation whenever
it is possible and mutually beneficial. But reconciliation
doesn't happen in every instance, no matter how much one
party may want it.

Sometimes efforts at reconciliation are not advisable.
In cases of physical, sexual, or other kinds of abuse, it may
not be safe to reconcile with the people who have wronged
us. Such people may still be dangerous to us, and it may be
better to avoid them. Or they may be in such a fragile con-
dition that confronting them with the past might devastate
them. There are times when it is wisest to let "bygones be
bygones," at least as far as confrontation and reconciliation

are concerned. However, it is never necessary or advisable to bypass the process of forgiveness.

When the Other Person Is Dead

Sometimes reconciliation is not possible because the other person is no longer living. The most common example is when we want to be reconciled to a parent who has died. There may, however, be ways to apply at least the dynamics of confrontation, even in such instances.

- Glen* went to his father's grave. There he poured out his heart about the things that had happened between them and how Glen wished things could have been. "I don't know if he could hear me," Glen said. "I guess it doesn't really matter. I was able to say the things I needed to say."

- Maria* took a large, framed portrait of her father down from the wall and spoke to it. "I remember gazing intently at every feature of his face," she said, "like I was trying to look into his soul." She did this a number of times over a period of months. Finally she was able to say, "Dad, I forgive you."

- Art* went back to his childhood home, a rustic cottage in the woods. He explained to the current owners that he had lived there as a boy and wanted to see the place again. They gave him permission to stroll through the woods. As he walked, he "talked" to his long-dead parents.

- Felicia* wrote a lengthy obituary about her parents. While she recalled the bad treatment she had received, she was also able to reflect on happy memories. That in itself was healing. In her days of pain, she had been able to remember nothing but the hurtful memories.

- Andrea* asked a married couple in her church, a couple she knew well and respected deeply, to sit in as surrogate parents. Then she talked through with them some of what she had experienced from her real parents.

Does there seem to be an element of make-believe in these techniques? I am not contending that these exercises are the same as actual, face-to-face confrontation and reconciliation. But they do help bring to bear some of the same dynamics in a way that helps advance the process of forgiveness.

Besides, in many cases what we really need to deal with is not so much our literal, flesh-and-blood, present-day parents as it is the *memory picture*—our parents as they once were. Most of us carry around within us such a memory picture of those who hurt us. It may be that those people have changed in the intervening years—that the people who hurt us, in a sense, no longer exist. Our main need, in such a case, may not be to confront our parents as they are now but to confront them as they were then. The kinds of exercises described here can be excellent tools for doing that.

The Girl Who Found Peace

When confrontation and other attempts at reconciliation are thoughtfully planned, and our attitudes and expectations are properly adjusted, such efforts can be a great help to the healing process.

Lydia* is a woman who had been molested by her stepfather with the full knowledge of her mother. She and her therapist decided it would be important for her to confront her parents with the truth about what had happened and how it had affected her.

Lydia spent several days writing out what she wanted

to say and going over it with her therapist. She rehearsed it in her support group. Other members of the group even played the parts of her parents, giving Lydia a chance to practice handling different kinds of responses. When the day came, Lydia handled her part perfectly. She didn't get into blaming. She didn't lose control and get angry. She just told her parents, calmly and objectively, what she wanted them to know.

Neither parent responded. They just sat there and denied everything Lydia had said. They were quite pleasant and polite about it but were completely unyielding in their denial. When Lydia's therapist tried to talk to them about how they were responding, they shut that out as well.

But Lydia was prepared. She had gone into the session knowing they might deny everything. When it was over, she told the others in her group that she felt relieved, as if a tremendous weight had been lifted from her shoulders. "It was like I set the truth on the table, and they were free to do whatever they wanted with it," she said. "If they wanted to ignore it, that was their business. But at least I wasn't lugging it around by myself anymore."

Lydia's story shows how we can be at peace even when reconciliation isn't possible. Lydia was at peace. She felt the need to test if reconciliation might be possible. When it turned out not to be, she wasn't thrown off. She knew that forgiveness was separate from reconciliation. And she knew that whether or not she ever reconciled with her parents, she had forgiven them. She had done everything that was in her power to do. She was released from the burden of the past.

Those of us who have worked through the process of forgiveness have the deep satisfaction of knowing that we can survive emotional injury—and not only survive but flourish as well. No matter how deep the wound, no matter how bitter the pain, once we forgive, we are no longer victims or mere survivors. We are victors. We have fought through to the ultimate. We have learned to love.**

*Name has been changed.

**Reprinted from David Stoop and James Masteller, *Forgiving Our Parents, Forgiving Ourselves.* © 1991 by Dr. David Stoop. Published by Servant Publications, Box 8617, Ann Arbor, MI 48107. Used with permission.

Background Scripture: Luke 15:11-32; Rom. 12:17-18

David Stoop is the clinical director of the Minirth-Meier-Stoop Clinics in Southern California. James Masteller is a marriage and family therapist with the clinic.

▼▼▼

A Quick Look Ahead

- Forgiving ourselves requires letting go of shame feelings. Whether shame stems from sin or mistakes, it can debilitate our personal growth. We can learn to forgive ourselves.

- As Christians, we are ineffective when we believe we're worthless. As long as we waste our energy mentally beating ourselves, we limit the energy left for healthy personal growth. Our self-image suffers until we learn to forgive ourselves.

- The first step to God's forgiveness is confession. Self-forgiveness begins the same way.

- Love is a decision. We can choose to love ourselves, no matter what the past. Forgiving ourselves is a part of loving ourselves so we can love others.

---- 4 ----

Learning to Forgive Ourselves

by Jan Frye

HE REALLY had no reason to feel as he did. Hubie* had many talents. He could lead the congregational singing. He could teach a Sunday School class just as well as a regular teacher. If he would, he could probably have even become a decent preacher.

The small church he attended needed multitalented people like Hubie. But he wouldn't use any of his gifts except in "extreme emergencies." Hubie just didn't feel he was worthy enough.

Hubie was saved. He had been gloriously converted in his mid-20s out of a hard life—hard-drinkin', hard-fightin', hard-to-survive. And he had been wondrously sanctified a short time afterward. Few people have walked in the way of holiness as beautifully as Hubie.

But Hubie had one point of shame that held him back. In his life before conversion, he had put several tattoos on his body. He had them everywhere. The one across the back of his hand was highly visible whenever Hubie was in front of the congregation. He was embarrassed. He was ashamed. He found it hard to forgive himself for his past. The tattoo reminded him of his sinful life, and he didn't want the congregation to see his shame.

If Hubie had learned to forgive himself as God had, he would have been free to serve God more fully in that small church.

Self-forgiveness is not a denial of guilt or of blame. When we forgive ourselves, we are not saying we did nothing wrong or were innocent victims—any more than divine forgiveness says we never sinned. Self-forgiveness does not necessarily eliminate the results of our misdeeds or lead to reconciliation.

Forgiving ourselves requires letting go of shame feelings. Whether shame stems from sin or mistakes, it can debilitate our personal growth. However, living with a constant sense of self-blame is unnecessary. We can learn to forgive ourselves.

Why Do We Need to Forgive Ourselves?

Forgiving ourselves is the right thing to do. Jesus Christ came to earth to teach and model forgiveness. Although we can expect to feel sadness and regret as consequences for some of our failures, we do not have to continually experience paralyzing guilt and shame. Forgiving ourselves is a positive step in the right direction.

Forgiving ourselves encourages us. To forgive is to value the person above the sin or mistake. It is a characteristic so beautifully evident in Jesus' encounter with the woman at the well, yet sadly lacking when we think of our own shortcomings. I know many fine Christians who wouldn't think of living with grudges and unkind words toward others but are constantly hard on themselves. One woman said, "Every time I think of how I missed my son's football game when he was 11, I still kick myself." What is going on here? Are we afraid we'll become prideful if we treat ourselves with the same respect we want from others? Perhaps we simply don't know how to live without feeling shame.

As Christians, we are ineffective when we believe we're worthless. As long as we waste our energy mentally beating ourselves, we limit the energy left for healthy, personal growth. It's possible to convince others we're OK, but we know the truth. Deep down, our self-image suffers until we learn to forgive ourselves.

Forgiving ourselves frees us to focus on others. As long as we're convinced others wouldn't like us if they knew our failures, we can't love them as Jesus does. The cleansing of a degrading attitude toward ourselves frees us to live out the fruits of the Spirit.

When we accept Christ's forgiveness and forgive ourselves, we are free to love. Instead of competition and comparison, we can find satisfaction in the achievements of others and enter into genuinely caring relationships.

Once we have accepted God's forgiveness, self-forgiveness erases shame with what the apostle Paul calls "godly sorrow" (2 Cor. 7:10). Moving from the false security of psychological shame to the uncharted waters of godly sorrow is a bit like flying from one trapeze to another. For one terrifying moment, we must give up our grasp on the only thing supporting us—in order to move on to something new. No matter how frightened we are, we cannot know the freedom of loving unless we let go of shame.

My friend Audrey asked, "Without shame, what would I do?" For one thing, moving into self-forgiveness through godly sorrow opens a door for us to stop thinking about our failures. Instead of living in extremes, we can have the freedom to do something creative and beneficial with our lives. The power of forgiveness motivates us to responsible action.

What Happens if We Don't Forgive Ourselves?

When shame builds over time, we become stuck in

shame-based living. We start to believe something is fundamentally wrong with us, that we are to blame. We doubt we can be forgiven for the things we've done. The shame we feel over a past event can rob us of the satisfaction of a new achievement. We never feel good enough. Soon, shame paralyzes us and fear immobilizes us.

Our shame can make us feel controlled and unloved, like a helpless child being beaten by a drunken adult. Our helplessness in the face of this shame and unnecessary self-anger can drive us to unhealthy forms of compensation. We may live a defensive lifestyle of extremes, leaving the path of personal growth for the destructive detours of workaholism, substance abuse, or addictions to food, sex, or spending. We may keep ourselves immersed in activities or shut off from others. We tend to live in fear that others might detect our shame and learn the truth about who we really are.

How Do We Find Forgiveness—
Especially if Others Won't Forgive Us?

It doesn't matter if others embrace us or throw tomatoes at us, self-forgiveness can still occur. Other people may react to our failures, but their reactions shouldn't keep us from forgiving ourselves.

A wise pastor once told me the first step to God's forgiveness is confession. Self-forgiveness begins the same way.

Steps to Forgiving Ourselves

1. Confess by stating the issue that needs to be forgiven.

By expressing our confession clearly, we can focus on the source of the shame. For example, a woman called me recently and confessed that she felt shame over some issues she needed to deal with one by one. "I have made poor decisions in the last few years," she admitted. "I ran away from home as a teen. I conceived a child while single. I married the baby's abusive father. When he hit me, I hit him back."

This is naming a confession, placing the truth up front to work with it and grow from it. Repentance for the poor actions follows confession. We can then depend on God's help to not repeat such behavior in the future.

2. *Wherever possible, do what is necessary to make amends for past failures.*

Once we have made all restitution possible, we can take the first steps out of the nagging shame of the past. The woman who confessed years of poor decisions could tell her husband she wishes she hadn't hit him and could let him know how she has decided to stay safe in the future. Also, she repaired a tabletop she had damaged in her anger at her husband.

3. *Explore the roots of our shame.*

Exploring the roots of shame with a professional may offer long-term benefits. But we can each begin by asking, "What am I avoiding in the present by hanging on to my shame?"

Recently, I watched a rerun of the sitcom "All in the Family." In one scene, Archie and Edith Bunker stood in the kitchen as Archie said, "The reason I'm fat, dear Edith, is because you feed me too much!"

Edith responded weakly, "Oh, Archie, I didn't mean to make you fat. I'm so sorry." If Edith explored the roots of her shame response, she might admit she was taking responsibility for things she should not have been. Then she might say, "Archie, I hear you say you're fat because I feed you too much, but I am not responsible for the food you put in your mouth."

How about the young man I know who requires himself to make straight A's, to always dress well, and to never disappoint others? When he makes a mistake, he could explore the roots of his shame by recognizing his unrealistic expectation toward perfectionism. He might learn, then, to be satisfied when he knows he has done his best.

As we explore the roots of our shame, we can determine to work on our vulnerable areas.

4. *Express our feelings and choose to use them as indicators for change.*

We may say something such as, "I still feel angry when I remember how my alcoholic mother yelled at me. My feelings overwhelmed me. To this day I feel shame when I don't know what to do. I realize I can't change the past, but right now I'm feeling overwhelmed. Rather than feeling ashamed, I will take this opportunity to move beyond my feelings of inadequacy and shame."

5. *State the decision of self-forgiveness.*

We can express our decision to forgive ourselves in a prayer, a drawing, or a personal journal. We can tell it to a trusted friend, a mirror, a tape recorder, or a counselor. Or we can express it in any other creative, measurable way. I know a teenager who listed specific issues of self-forgiveness on index cards and then ceremoniously burned them one by one in the fireplace.

Forgiveness is a thought, an act of the will, and an attitude. But forgiveness is not necessarily a feeling. We might say something like, "I know that forgiving myself means admitting I have limitations and cannot always please people. I hereby forgive myself for feeling shame over this. I choose to do myself a favor and let go of my shame. I choose at this moment to allow this experience to help me grow."

Most people today realize that love is a decision. We can choose to love and respect ourselves—no matter what we feel about the past—because God has loved us first.

Forgiving ourselves is a part of loving ourselves so that we can love others.

Over a lifetime, we've stuffed our accumulated shame feelings, one by one, into a mental backpack. Every time we experience a new shame or relive the sting of a previous shame, we toss all those feelings into the imaginary backpack. We lug the ever-increasing, heavy load around each day. But when we forgive ourselves, we can imagine throwing the whole backpack into a Dumpster and walking away, shame free. With no backpack to stow future shame, we can deal with self-forgiveness as an ongoing way of life.

We can trust our own forgiveness. If feelings of doubt return, we can confess the feelings as real and then relax, remembering when and where we forgave ourselves. I don't understand why disturbing feelings sometimes resurface after self-forgiveness. Perhaps our emotions tend to return to old, familiar patterns. Perhaps Jesus allows those feelings to remind us how much He wants us to continue turning to Him with any feelings or desires that trouble us. After all, He said, "Come to me, all you who are weary and burdened, and I will give you rest" (Matt. 11:28).

Once we have truly forgiven ourselves, we can train our minds to replay a mental videotape of self-forgiveness. We can remember throwing our shame-filled backpack into the Dumpster, and we can rest in that truth. Then we can look forward to the future—free, full of adventure, full of hope. And, best of all, we can focus on loving others.

*Name has been changed.

Background Scripture: Matt. 11:28; John 8:3-11

Jan Frye is a counselor in Olathe, Kans.

▼▼▼

A Quick Look Ahead

- To restore peace in our most important relationship, we can choose to forgive God. Forgive God? That we need to be forgiven by God is without question. That God needs to be forgiven by us borders on blasphemy. Why forgive God?

- Some need to forgive God because they blame Him for all human tragedy. Others need to forgive God because they resent Him for not allowing a loved one to live. Some need to forgive God because they blame Him for creating them with flaws.

- Perhaps a better way to describe what it means to forgive God is to say that we need to *reconcile* with God. The term "reconciliation" literally means "to completely change." It carries with it the idea of removing the barriers that separate two individuals so that the relationship can be changed from a state of estrangement to a state of closeness.

- The bottom line of forgiving God is the removal of barriers that prevent us from trusting Him—barriers of silence, resentment, or forgetfulness.

5

Forgiving God?

by Charles D. Kelley

WHAT CAN A young woman do with her bitter feelings toward God when she finds herself experiencing her third miscarriage in 15 months? What can parents do with their profound anger toward God when they learn that their baby boy has Down's syndrome? How can an elderly man not blame God when he discovers that he has Parkinson's disease? How can a victim of a horrible car accident or a cruel rape effectively come to grips with the truth that God does care, He is all-powerful, yet He permits awful tragedies?

To restore peace in our most important relationship, we can choose to forgive God.

Forgive God? That we need to be forgiven by God is without question. That God needs to be forgiven by us borders on blasphemy. Why forgive God? No one has the right to pardon God, for He has not sinned against anyone. Yet many of us may need to go through a process with God that resembles forgiveness. Not because God has sinned and needs to be pardoned, but because we treat

Him as if He has. Even though God doesn't need to be pardoned, we may need to forgive Him.*

Why We Blame God

Let's take a look at a few reasons why some people need to forgive God:

Some need to forgive God because they blame Him for all human tragedy. There's an old story about a Jewish tailor who met a rabbi on his way out of the synagogue.

"Well, and what have you been doing in the synagogue, Lev Ashram?" inquired the rabbi.

"I was saying prayers, Rabbi."

"Fine, and did you confess your sins?"

"Yes, Rabbi, I confessed my little sins."

"Your little sins?"

"Yes, I confessed that sometimes I cut cloth on the short side and cheat on a yard of wool by a couple of inches."

"You said that to God, Lev Ashram?"

"Yes, Rabbi, and more. I said, 'Lord, I cheat on a piece of cloth; You let little babies die. But I am going to make You a deal. You forgive my little sins, and I'll forgive Your big ones.'"

Over the centuries God has been accused of many big sins. He has been labeled as cruel, partial, sadistic, uncaring, and powerless. If God is good, why does He allow human suffering? Is it really in His will that half of the world's population starve? How can a gracious God permit countless babies to be born with severe birth defects? Why would God allow a young father to accidentally run over and crush his two-year-old child while backing his car out of the driveway?

---

*Throughout this chapter, even though we use the phrase "forgive God," we realize that we are really coming to understand and remove any barriers on our part that keep us from experiencing the fullness of God's love.

To forgive God is to look these tough questions right in the eye. To come to grips with scriptural truth about God's love, power, and sovereignty. Then to fully submit to His will.

Others need to forgive God because they resent Him for not allowing a loved one to live. Recently, our friends lost their 55-year-old mother. Her cancer had been diagnosed nearly two years before. The initial, exploratory surgery indicated that the disease had spread rapidly and death would happen soon.

An army of believers began to pray. To the doctor's amazement, she improved rapidly and was soon in remission. How the Church rejoiced! This gifted and godly woman would continue to live a fruitful life. It was so right.

Suddenly, right after Christmas, the cancer reappeared. More prayers were offered to the Lord—but to no avail. She declined rapidly and died.

"Why?" demanded our friends. "Her life was so productive. Why did she have to die? How come God permits that good-for-nothing grump over there to live and yet insists that Mom die? It isn't fair! It isn't right!"

What could they do? They could either let their anger fester, or they could choose to forgive God. They did the latter.

To forgive God is to choose to honestly identify one's negative feelings toward God, verbalize them to Him, and then release them to His care.

Some need to forgive God because they blame Him for creating them with flaws. Since early childhood I have struggled with a speech impediment. There have been times when I have been unable to answer the phone, order a hamburger, or even say my name.

I sought help from a professional speech coach. He said I was a hopeless case.

I tried the technique of inflicting pain on myself whenever I sensed the onset of speech obstruction, in order to distract my subconscious mind and free my tongue to speak fluently. It worked, but I soon realized that such behavior was actually a greater bondage in itself.

I went to a Christian psychiatrist who prescribed an antidepressant drug that did not help the problem. For eight months I went through counseling, analyzing the deep feelings of anger I have harbored toward the important people of my past. That helped some, but not much.

In desperation, I even asked a fellow pastor to expose and expel the "demon of stuttering" so that I could be effectively used by God in a proclamation ministry. Yet I still stutter.

The embarrassment and pain that a stutterer experiences in the middle of a speech obstruction is devastating. Without a doubt, the larger frustration comes in trying to answer the question—Why? Answers simply aren't there.

Several years ago I took a long walk to talk this matter over with God. "Lord," I pleaded, "either take away my desire to preach or take away my stuttering. It's not fair for You to plant a passion within my heart to proclaim Your truth and then to see to it that I stumble all over my tongue in the process."

I kept walking and praying, hoping to sense some sort of answer. Nothing. More walking and praying. Still nothing. Finally, I declared to the Father, "Lord, if You want me to preach, I'll preach. And if You want me to stutter, I'll stutter. I don't understand, but if You can use a stammering preacher, here am I. Use me. I'm willing to stutter for Your glory." I still preach. I still stutter. But God is using me.

What did I do that evening while walking and praying? I openly admitted my feelings toward God, talked it over with Him, quit blaming Him for my problems, and yielded myself to His service. Among other things, I forgave God.

To Reconcile with God

Perhaps a better way to describe what it means to forgive God is to say that we need to *reconcile* with God. The term "reconciliation" literally means "to completely change." It carries with it the idea of removing the barriers that separate two individuals, so that the relationship can be changed from a state of estrangement to a state of closeness.

For us to reconcile with God is not to be confused with the fact that He has reconciled us to himself. God has already removed all the barriers that prevented Him from offering us forgiveness.

As Paul wrote to the church in Colosse, "Once you were alienated from God and were enemies in your minds because of your behavior. But now he has reconciled you by Christ's physical body through death to present you holy in his sight, without blemish and free from accusation" (Col. 1:21-22). Paul is saying that God completely changed our status from aliens to citizens, from enemies to friends. Then He offered us forgiveness. We were simply the object of reconciliation, not the initiators. God did all the reconciling.

But in another sense we can reconcile with God. When a barrier separates us from God, we must identify it and the conditions that have permitted the barrier to remain. Our attitude must be completely changed and the barrier removed. When we do that, we reconcile with God.

Breaking Down the Barriers

The bottom line of forgiving God is the removal of

barriers that prevent us from trusting Him. Let's take a look at a few:

The barrier of silence. When a human relationship is strained, it is natural for both parties to avoid communication with the other. Yet, without communication, the removal of barriers is impossible.

The same is true in our relationship with God, with one major exception—God is always available to communicate with us. The real question is—are we willing to talk with Him?

The Bible is filled with examples of people who struggled with many of the same issues we do. Take the Psalms. David was so overwhelmed by his enemies and felt so completely abandoned by God that he broke the barrier of silence with God by writing out this prayer: "My God, my God, why have you forsaken me? Why are you so far from saving me, so far from the words of my groaning? O my God, I cry out by day, but you do not answer" (Ps. 22:1-2).

Have you ever said something like that to God? I have. There have been times when I've been so exasperated with a situation that I have echoed David's words.

Don't misunderstand. It's not particularly virtuous for us to vent our frustration at God, but it is infinitely better to communicate our frustrated feelings toward God than to remain silent and become bitter. But let's not forget that the goal in such communication is resolution, not merely emotional relief.

The barrier of resentment. This is perhaps the most difficult barrier to get rid of, for it requires us to acknowledge that we are actually bitter toward God. This is tough for most of us, for who wants to admit that he has the audacity to hold a grudge against God?

Did you notice how David acknowledged his anger with God? He didn't pull any punches. He felt God had been ignoring his prayers—even though he believed otherwise. So he poured out all the emotions of his heart to the Father.

We need to do the same thing. When we're upset with God for any reason, we must come to grips with our hostile feelings and describe them to Him. I find that a pad of paper and a pen are helpful tools in this process. I answer the following questions on a sheet of paper:

- Do I know of anyone I need to forgive?
- Do I harbor any resentment toward God?
- What do I need to do to resolve that conflict now?

Then I write out a prayer to the Lord describing my thoughts and feelings. I make sure not to leave my prayer session until I have acknowledged, confessed, and dealt with all known feelings of bitterness toward God.

The barrier of forgetfulness. A wise man once said, "It is required more often for men to be reminded than to be informed." Through the regular study of God's Word, we must remind ourselves of what God is really like. He does care. He can intervene. He is in full control.

This is how the psalmist resolved his conflict with God. "You are enthroned as the Holy One; you are the praise of Israel" (Ps. 22:3). David redirected his focus from his predicament to the character of God, and in so doing was able to relinquish his bitterness. Then he could peacefully trust God again.

Scripture doesn't answer all the specifics of our "why" questions, but it does sharpen our focus on the One who knows why. Then we can rest in His assurance.

Choosing Bitterness or Trust?

Let me tell two true stories. Both contain tragedy and the need to forgive God. Yet, in these stories we see two different responses and two different outcomes.

Charlie is an 80-year-old bachelor who lives in a retirement home. He is plagued not only with cancer and emphysema but also with the reputation of being rude, bitter, and angry. He frequently tells his fellow residents that he wants to die.

Recently, he was engaged in a rather lively conversation with the chaplain. "I'm tired of living. Why can't I die?" Charlie demanded.

"Well," replied the chaplain, "if you're ready to die and have made peace with the Lord—"

"I don't want to have anything to do with God!" he interrupted. "Years ago I believed in God. Then my mother got sick. I prayed that God would heal her, but she died. And I've never forgiven Him for it. I hate God. I don't want to have anything to do with Him!"

Is there any wonder that Charlie wants to die?

Writer and speaker Ann Kiemel tells the story of a car ride with a young couple and their little girl, Paula. The child wore braces on her legs, the result of cerebral palsy.

Sitting on Ann's lap, Paula said, "Ann, I have a new baby brother."

Seeing no baby, Ann asked, "You do? Where is he?"

Paula's mother turned around from the front seat and said, "Ann, Paula doesn't understand. God did give us a little baby boy a few months ago, but he lived for only a few weeks."

She went on to describe that after he died, they became very angry. They asked God all the "why" questions.

"And, Ann," she concluded, "we still don't have all the answers, but we're working it through. Our anger and pain have gradually been replaced by His peace. Even though we don't understand why He took our baby away, we do understand that because we have Paula, He's given us a ministry to other parents of children with cerebral palsy. We're reaching scores of people for Christ who might never have been reached otherwise, and we're thankful to God for that."

Two different crises. Two different responses. Two very different results.

We all experience tragedy. How we respond to God during tragedy will, to a large degree, determine if we will emerge from that crisis weakened or strengthened.

When life hurts, we have two choices. We can become embittered and resentful, building barriers between ourselves and our Heavenly Father. Or we can tear down the barriers, surrender our concept of how life should be, and forgive God. Then we will discover that He has been waiting there to reconcile with us all the time.

Background Scripture: Job 16:9-14; 42:1-6; Ps. 22:1-3; Col. 1:21-22

Charles D. Kelley is the senior pastor of a church in Corvallis, Oreg.

▼▼▼

A Quick Look Ahead

- Unfortunately, most of the people we meet focus primarily on outward appearance. Focusing on outward appearance gives us a quite different picture of the worth of a human being than God sees. Our self-worth should not be founded upon our appearance. Instead, we should see that we have worth because God values us.

- Most of us at some time in our lives feel "too" something—too fat, too thin, too tall, too short. Body image is a very important part of self-concept.

- We should alter those parts of our physical appearance that we can change, if they are causing us to feel badly about ourselves. But we should never make changes to *become* acceptable. No diet, exercise program, or clothes will give us self-worth.

- Our reactions to the physical appearance of others should be directed by the Spirit. The Body of Believers should accept, and even celebrate, differences in personal appearance. Our church has people of all colors, shapes, and sizes.

6

God Looks on the Inside, but I Have to Look in the Mirror

by Richard A. Fish

IT WAS A LOVELY, clear day atop a beautiful mountain in the Swiss Alps. My brother, Don, and I shared a scenic overlook with an attractive young woman full of travel questions. As a seasoned traveler, I always feel good when I can draw on many years of experience to assist someone. But each time I tried to help her, she directed her questions back to Don.

After several frustrating exchanges, it suddenly dawned on me. Even as a middle-aged man, my brother was better looking than me. It was just like when we were teenagers! Like it or not, physical appearance does affect how we feel about ourselves, because it affects how people react to us.

This is by no means a problem unique to our own era. In one passage of Scripture the Lord tells Samuel, "Do not look on his appearance or on the height of his stature . . . for the Lord does not see as mortals see; they look on the outward appearance, but the Lord looks on the heart" (1 Sam. 16:7, NRSV).

Unfortunately, most of the people we meet, like the woman in the Swiss Alps, focus primarily on the outward appearance.

Early Influences

The link between physical appearance and self-concept can start shortly after birth. When I visited our first daughter in the hospital nursery, I noticed the babies with hair got picked up and held much more often than the bald ones. We know that physical contact is very important to developing a sense of well-being, and the process begins long before a child can walk and talk.

Furthermore, children can be set up for rejection by others, even by well-meaning parents. It isn't fair, but a chubby child is more likely to be chosen last in games and other activities. Ironically, loving parents may overfeed their children. As adults, some of us still battle inner voices that say, "Clean up your plate," or "Have a second helping."

Some young people and adults still have echoes playing in their heads with negative words about their appearance: "I'm ugly." "I'm a fat slob." "I have ears like Dumbo." A good parent is careful not to feed this damaging self-talk with negative comments about a child's appearance. It is much better for a child to remember the voice of a parent saying he or she looks handsome or beautiful.

Teenagers' physical appearance affects their self-concepts more dramatically than at other ages, but it is not just a teenage problem. We "older folks" don't outgrow our concerns about appearance. It is not uncommon for us to consider, *What will they think if I wear this outfit?* Or, *What will someone say if I grow a beard?* Or what adult doesn't worry that he or she has gained too many pounds?

Focusing on outward appearances gives us a quite different picture of the worth of a human being than God sees. Our self-worth should not be founded upon our appearance. Instead, we should see that we have worth because God values us.

One writer has painted the picture this way:

> The Scriptures indicate that human beings are special to God in a number of ways. They are the apex of God's creation (Gen. 1), created in the image of God (Gen. 1:26-27), with each of us having the potential of becoming a child of God (John 1:12-13). In the Old Testament the Psalmist marveled that we were created "a little lower than the angels" (Ps. 8:5) and are given a special purpose by God (Gen. 1:18). The New Testament writers, too, acknowledge that human beings are a creation special to God. We are the objects of God's redemptive purposes in this world (John 3:16). As redeemed people, we even have angels watching over us (Heb. 1:14; Ps. 91:11-12; Dan. 6:22; compare Matt. 4:11) and Jesus himself preparing a place for us in eternity (John 14:1-3).
>
> Clearly, humankind has worth to God, individually and as a race.[1]

Culture and Acceptance

Most of us at some time in our lives feel "too" something—too fat, too thin, too tall, too short. Body image is a very important part of self-concept. Advertising is designed to make us dissatisfied with our physical appearance. Models are thinner or more muscular or better dressed than most people. We spend billions of dollars on diet programs, exercise equipment, and expensive clothing trying to look like something we are not. Beautiful women with perfect hair even urge us to buy expensive hair products because we're "worth it."

Yet the writer of Romans warns us, "Do not conform any longer to the pattern of this world, but be transformed by the renewing of your mind" (Rom. 12:2).

Another writer shows us clearly the "pattern of this world" when he writes:

> The contrast between society's foundation of self-worth and the biblical base for self-esteem is startling. It's like sand compared to rock. The societal foundation of self-worth is based on power and put-downs. Our eyes are turned to things and people. We're always comparing ourselves with others to see how we look. We're encouraged to put others down so we can look better. This gets us into an endless rat race. But Scripture turns our eyes to God. It bases self-esteem on love and the stable base of God's high acceptance.[2]

As Christians, we will be happier if we accept ourselves physically, care for our bodies as the temple of God (1 Cor. 3:16), but not become obsessed with our appearance (1 Tim. 4:8). "Your beauty should not come from outward adornment, such as braided hair and the wearing of gold jewelry and fine clothes. Instead, it should be that of your inner self, the unfading beauty of a gentle and quiet spirit, which is of great worth in God's sight" (1 Pet. 3:3-4).

The story of "Fat Albert" is an illustration of acceptance:

> "See Fat Albert, the world's fattest man," blared the prerecorded sales pitch. "He is real and he is alive and he weighs 870 pounds!"
>
> I walked up the platform's well-worn steps, half expecting "Fat Albert" to be a stuffed doll or some other deception. I was truly surprised as I peered behind the three-sided partition and saw an enormous man sitting on a small seat . . .
>
> Fat Albert said he was born in a small town in

Mississippi. A genetic defect caused him to accumulate his abnormal weight and yes, indeed, he did weigh 870 pounds.

I stepped to the side as other people came into the booth. . . . He patiently answered their questions and had a ready, humorous reply for the taunts a scoffer hurled.

I was about to leave when one of the teenagers in the group asked him how he felt being the world's fattest man.

"Well, we're all made in God's image, aren't we?" Albert said. "And we all come in different shapes and sizes. God made me the way I am for a purpose, and He made you the way you are for a purpose. The Bible says that the body is going to die, and the spirit is going to live on, so *it is more important how we live than how we look*" (emphasis added).[3]

The Right Perspective

We should alter those parts of our physical appearance that we can change, if they are causing us to feel badly about ourselves. If we can lose a few pounds, we should lose them. If we can exercise our way into better shape, we should do it. If we can buy a few clothes and dress in style, it will help us feel better. But we should never make changes to *become* acceptable. Rather, we should do it because we *have* self-worth. No diet, exercise program, or clothes will give us self-worth. That can only come from seeing ourselves as God sees us—worthwhile beings created in His image.

At the same time, we should accept those parts of our physical appearance that we cannot change. Whatever we perceive ourselves to be—too tall, too short; too fat, too thin; feet too clumsy or too dainty; ears too big or too small; nose too long or too pug—God made us that way for a purpose.

We should not let other people define our attractiveness as persons. People who seem to have a need to point out our inadequate physical characteristics are not helping our self-esteem. We should spend less time with critical individuals and more time with people who accept us as we are.

Our perception of how our bodies look controls how we feel about our bodies. It is important to have a realistic view of our physical appearance. I knew a student years ago who had an unreal view of herself physically. Margaret* was seen by most people as exceptionally beautiful, yet she thought of herself as ugly.

When she passed other students on the sidewalk, she would look down and not respond to greetings because she was uncomfortable being noticed. Soon others began to think of her as conceited. In the safety of a small group, she came to realize that she was not ugly. Her view of herself changed to a more accurate picture.

Even the process of aging is something we must learn to accept. Our eyes might become dimmer. Our ears may not pick up sounds well. Our legs may not carry us without complaint. But none of this diminishes our worth as human beings. God uses nothing of our outside to judge our value. We should treat ourselves as well.

Self-acceptance is still the key—whether we choose to color the gray hair or not. Old age gives a chance for the inner beauty to shine through as the surface beauty fades.

How Should the Church React?

Our reactions to the physical appearance of others should be directed by the Spirit and be full of acceptance and support. Men as well as women tend to be uneasy about their appearance. Part of our responsibility of love is to help others feel comfortable about themselves. And part of our obligation to others is to notice changes and give positive affirmation.

The body of believers should accept, and even celebrate, differences in personal appearance. Our church has people of all colors, shapes, and sizes. Some dress in the latest fashions, others in last year's model. Some have hair, some don't. Amazingly, God seems to overlook all the differences and see right to the heart. We should take this hint from God.

Whatever our age and whatever our physical attributes, we should try to see ourselves and others as God does. Jesus taught us:

> Look at the birds of the air; they do not sow or reap or store away in barns, and yet your heavenly Father feeds them. Are you not much more valuable than they? . . . And why do you worry about clothes? See how the lilies of the field grow. . . . If that is how God clothes the grass of the field, which is here today and tomorrow is thrown into the fire, will he not much more clothe you? *(Matt. 6:26, 28, 30).*

The next time we look in the mirror, let's try to see ourselves as God does.

*Name has been changed.

1. Josh McDowell, *Building Your Self-Esteem* (Wheaton, Ill.: Tyndale House, 1984), 42.

2. Gene Van Note, ed., *Building Self-Esteem* (Kansas City: Beacon Hill Press of Kansas City, 1982), 10.

3. Doug Vinson, "Fat Albert," *Moody Monthly* (July / August 1981), 25.

Background Scripture: John 7:24; 1 Sam. 16:7; 1 Pet. 3:3-4

Richard A. Fish is a clinical psychologist at Eastern Nazarene College in Quincy, Mass.

▼▼▼

A Quick Look Ahead

- Like many teenage girls, I found much of my identity in my appearance. Adolescence revolved around my outside image. Being pretty meant I had lots of dates and a wide circle of friends.

- I asked the nurse for a mirror. Her refusal to give me a mirror only fueled my irrational determination. *If she wouldn't give me a mirror,* I reasoned, *it must be worse than I imagined.*

- I propped myself on my elbows, and through lips that could barely move, hissed, "You don't love me! Now that I'm not pretty anymore, you just don't love me!"

- Nothing could have prepared me for what I saw. An image that resembled a giant scraped knee, oozing and bright pink, looked out at me. My eyes and lips were crusted and swollen. Hardly a patch of skin, ear to ear, had escaped the trauma.

7

Through a Father's Eyes

by Lonni Collins Pratt

I SAW THE CAR just before it hit me. I seemed to float. Then darkness smashed my senses.

I came to in an ambulance. Opening my eyes, I could see only shreds of light through my bandaged, swollen eyelids. I didn't know it then, but small particles of gravel and dirt were embedded in my freckled, 16-year-old face. As I tried to touch it, someone tenderly pressed my arm down and whispered, "Lie still."

A wailing siren trailed distantly, and I slipped into unconsciousness. My last thoughts were a desperate prayer, *Dear God, not my face, please . . .*

Like many teenage girls, I found much of my identity in my appearance. Adolescence revolved around my outside image. Being pretty meant I had lots of dates and a wide circle of friends.

Ever since childhood, people had related to me differently than they related to less-attractive girls. I had grown to depend on my looks. When I was four, Santa had picked me out of 600 kids to be his helper. Why? Because I was pretty. I had gotten out of more than one jam by batting my eyes and tilting my head just right so that the light caught my red hair.

My father doted on me. He had four sons, but only one daughter. I remember one Sunday in particular. As we got out of the car at church, my brothers—a scruffy three-some in corduroy and cowlicks—ran ahead. Mom had stayed home with the sick baby.

I was gathering my small purse, church school papers, and Bible. Dad opened the door. I looked up at him, convinced in my seven-year-old heart that he was more hand-some and smelled better than any daddy anywhere.

He extended his hand to me with a twinkle in his eye and said, "A hand, my lady?" Then he swept me up into his arms and told me how pretty I was. "No father has ever loved a little girl more than I love you," he said.

In my child's heart, which didn't really understand a father's love, I thought it was my pretty dress and face he loved.

A few weeks before the accident, I had won first place in a local pageant, making me the festival queen. Dad didn't say much. He just stood beside me with his arm over my shoulders, beaming with pride. Once more, I was his pretty little girl; and I basked in the warmth of his love and acceptance.

About this same time, I made a personal commitment to Christ. In the midst of student council, honor society, pageants, and parades, I was beginning a relationship with God.

My Parents Hid the Mirror

In the hours immediately after my accident, I drifted in and out of consciousness. Whenever my mind cleared even slightly, I wondered about my face. I was bleeding in-ternally and had a severe concussion, but it never occurred to me that my concern with appearance was dispropor-tionate.

The next morning, although I couldn't open my eyes more than a slit, I asked the nurse for a mirror. "You just concern yourself with getting well, young lady," she said, not looking at my face as she took my blood pressure.

Her refusal to give me a mirror only fueled my irrational determination. *If she wouldn't give me a mirror,* I reasoned, *it must be worse than I imagined.* My face felt tight and itchy. It burned sometimes and ached other times. I didn't touch it, though, because my doctor told me that might cause infection.

My parents also battled to keep mirrors away. As my body healed internally and strength returned, I became increasingly difficult.

At one point, for the fourth time in less than an hour, I pleaded for a mirror. Five days had passed since the accident.

Angry and beaten down, Dad snapped, "Don't ask again! I said no, and that's it!"

I wish I could offer an excuse for what I said. I propped myself on my elbows, and through lips that could barely move, hissed, "You don't love me! Now that I'm not pretty anymore, you just don't love me!"

Dad looked as if someone had knocked the wind out of him. He slumped into a chair and put his head in his hands. My mother walked over and put her hand on his shoulder as he tried to control his tears. I collapsed against the pillows.

I didn't ask my parents for a mirror again. Instead, I waited until the housekeeper was straightening my room the next morning. My curtain was drawn as if I were taking a sponge bath. "Could you get me a mirror, please?" I asked. "I must have mislaid mine." After a little searching, she found one and discreetly handed it to me around the curtain.

Nothing could have prepared me for what I saw. An image that resembled a giant scraped knee, oozing and bright pink, looked out at me. My eyes and lips were crusted and swollen. Hardly a patch of skin, ear to ear, had escaped the trauma.

My father arrived a little later with magazines and homework tucked under his arm. He found me staring into the mirror. Prying my fingers one by one from the mirror, he said, "It isn't important. This doesn't change anything that matters. No one will love you less."

Finally, he pulled the mirror away and tossed it into a chair. He sat on the edge of my bed, took me in his arms, and held me a long time.

"I know what you think," he said.

"You couldn't," I mumbled, turning away and staring out the window.

Ignoring my self-pity, he repeated, "This will not change anything." He put his hand on my arm, across an IV line. "The people who love you have seen you at your worst, you know."

"Right. Seen me with rollers or with cold cream, not with my face ripped off!"

He said. "I love you. Nothing will ever change that because it's you I love, not your outside. I've changed your diapers and watched your skin blister with chicken pox. I've wiped up your bloody noses and held your head while you threw up in the toilet. I've loved you when you weren't pretty."

He hesitated. "Yesterday you were ugly—not because of your skin, but because your behavior was ugly. But I'm here today, and I'll be here tomorrow. Fathers don't stop loving their children, no matter what life takes away. You will be blessed if life takes only your face."

I turned to my father, feeling he was merely saying

words. The right words, but spoken out of duty. Just polite lies.

"Look at me, Daddy," I said. "Look at me, and tell me you love me!"

I will never forget what happened next. As he looked into my battered face, his eyes filled with tears. Slowly, he leaned toward me, and with his eyes open, he gently kissed my scabbed, oozing lips. It was the same kiss that had tucked me in every night of my young life. The kiss that had warmed each morning.

Many years have passed. All that remains of my accident is a tiny indentation above one eyebrow. But my father's kiss, and what it taught me about accepting love, will never leave me.

Background Scripture: Prov. 17:17; Luke 11:10-12; 1 Cor. 13:4-7

Lonni Collins Pratt is a freelance writer in Lapeer, Mich.

▼▼▼

A Quick Look Ahead

- Many things are said that are better forgotten, but words have a life of their own. Once spoken, they can never be unspoken.

- In some homes, words are used as weapons to crush the human spirit. These verbal missiles attack almost anything attached to a person—possessions, behavior, appearance, intelligence, or even value as a person. In the same way radiation sickness destroys the immune system, toxic words destroy the spirit. In extreme form, it is called verbal abuse.

- Destructive criticism always weakens self-esteem and causes psychological pain.

- There are times when we need to give constructive guidance. We may even find it necessary to confront another person concerning irresponsible behavior. The point is not to avoid careful thinking and simply accept everything. The point is to make our evaluations helpful and not damage a person's self-image in the process.

8

Overcoming Criticism

by Les Parrott III

IN THE THIRD grade I read with amazement the legends attached to the life of Paul Bunyan. He was a mythical woodsman from the headwaters of the Mississippi River in Minnesota and was larger and more powerful than any other man in the woods. His voice made the birds stop singing and the leaves tremble. Everyone did what he commanded, except for one man.

That lone woodsman was given to critical attitudes and to streams of profanity that scandalized even the ears of rough-hewn lumbermen who usually took no notice of expletives. Paul Bunyan commanded him to stop his critical ways, but it did no good. He begged, cajoled, threatened, bribed—every means he knew—to stop the terrible bursts of offensive language, but to no avail. Bunyan then turned to violence. Although he pummeled the offender mercilessly, it did not change his language. Then something happened that changed everything.

One winter, it got cold enough in Minnesota to send the mercury in the thermometer to unmeasurable degrees of cold, far below zero on the Fahrenheit scale. The extreme cold "froze" each word instantly as it was spoken.

Watching these frozen words drop to the ground gave Paul Bunyan an idea. He ordered all of the frozen words of the offensive lumberman to be picked up and stacked in successive order, to await the coming of spring. When the bitter cold of winter gave way to the warming rays of the sun and the temperatures began to rise above the melting zone, Paul Bunyan made the lumberman sit down and listen to every expletive he had uttered all winter. According to the story, the man never said another critical word.

The Paul Bunyan story is myth, but it is both intriguing and frightening. Many things are said that are better forgotten, but words have a life of their own. Once spoken, they can never be unspoken. When we listen to ourselves, we sometimes hear what we do not like. Too often our conversations are weighed down with quick-frozen criticism and only lightly sprinkled with compliments.

Toxic Verbal Weapons

Shortly after midnight Saturday, April 26, 1986, routine maintenance was in progress at the Chernobyl nuclear power plant in the northeast corner of the Ukraine. An uncontrolled power surge raced through reactor No. 4, producing steam and hydrogen, which caused a massive explosion. A mile-high nuclear cloud hovered for 10 days over vast areas of the Soviet Union and Europe, releasing radioactive rain.

In the summer of 1993, I saw firsthand the devastation this event brought to the region and its people. On a humanitarian assignment, I was sent to Chernobyl to help those who had not been responsive to physical healing. I walked around in an abused landscape that will require many years to recover. I talked with suffering children. I listened to their desperate parents. I met with courageous doctors, and I saw what life was like in Chernobyl's "Dead Zone." Things will never be simple again for 2 million residents who are still exposed daily to high levels of radiation.

Reflecting on my emotional experience in Chernobyl's contaminated region and continuing my work as a counselor with troubled families in the United States, I have come to a fresh realization: As soil and air are poisoned by radiation, so the human heart and mind are poisoned by critical attitudes.

In some homes, words are used as weapons to crush the human spirit. These verbal missiles attack almost anything attached to a person—possessions, behavior, appearance, intelligence, or even value as a person. James says that the human tongue is "full of deadly poison" (3:8).

In the same way radiation sickness destroys the immune system, toxic words destroy the spirit. In extreme form, it is called verbal abuse. It comes through in statements such as: "You'll never amount to anything." "Can't you do anything right?" "You are the most disgusting little creep who ever walked the face of the earth." Verbal abuse, many experts claim, is just as destructive as physical abuse. The Apocrypha[1] says, "The blow of a whip raises a welt, but the blow of the tongue crushes bones."

Verbal toxicity, however, is often dispensed in subtle forms. For example, we sometimes camouflage our criticism in humor. People wriggle out of cruel statements by saying, "I was only joking." Or we shoot a poisonous dart of "helpful" advice that is actually meant as a clever putdown. Sometimes we withhold our attention to express our disapproval. As a Yiddish[2] proverb says, "If you're out to beat a dog, you're sure to find a stick." Regardless of its form, criticism poisons the human spirit much like a nuclear disaster poisons a country.

Avoid Toxic Talk

Destructive criticism always weakens self-esteem and

causes psychological pain. Like a sharp javelin, a critical attitude cuts relationships and lessens self-worth. Trying to be with a critical person is like walking across a bog. We never know when the ground may give way to a cold, nasty experience.

Since the pain of being criticized seems universal, it is somewhat surprising that most of us are so quick to criticize others, even the people who are closest to us and central to our happiness. We seem to have an irresistible urge to find fault. Some cynic has said, "We find fault with perfection itself." Here are a few suggestions for sidestepping the toxic verbal weapon of criticism.

Separate the person from the behavior. Place our interpersonal focus on what a person does, rather than on who we see him or her to be. This shift from the person to the behavior implies the use of adverbs (related to actions) rather than adjectives (related to qualities) when referring to persons. Thus, one might say a person "talked a great deal in the meeting," rather than that this person "is a loudmouth."

Observe rather than infer. Woodrow Wilson once said, in regard to criticism, "The thing to do is to supply light and not heat." Observation of what we see or hear in another person's behavior supplies that light. Conclusions based on what we hear or see, on the other hand, provide heat. Inferences and conclusions contaminate our conversations and destroy relationships.

Describe rather than judge. It has been said that the rule in carving holds good when applied to criticism: Never cut with a knife what can be cut with a spoon. The effort to describe represents a gentle process of reflecting a person's actions, while judgment refers to an evaluation of whether the person is good or bad, right or wrong. Instead of inferring and judging by saying, "You are so uncaring and conceited. You never want to know what I think," try observing and describing by saying, "I am disappointed. It feels like you are not considering my opinion on this."

Focus on the "here and now," not the "there and then." Feedback is most meaningful if given as soon as it is appropriate to do so. Holding down a critical comment is like putting it into a simmering stew that eventually boils. Repressed criticisms have a high rate of resurrection, and they often reappear uglier than ever before.

Share ideas, not advice. A little advice, like a little garlic, goes a long way. When people dole out advice before earning the right to give it, the advice comes off as a put-down, even when there is a genuine desire to help. Advice can stir up terrible pangs of guilt. The advice Job's friends gave him in his time of affliction, for example, only served to make him more miserable. Giving unsought advice is like giving a hammer to a person who may need a screwdriver—who needs it?

It's Our Decision

There are times when we need to give constructive guidance. We may even find it necessary to confront another person concerning irresponsible behavior. But how we express corrective guidance makes all the difference in whether a person will listen and act on it. The point is not to avoid careful thinking and simply accept everything. The point is to make our evaluations helpful and not damage a person's self-image in the process. The apostle Paul understood this when he wrote: "Therefore let us stop passing judgment on one another. Instead, make up your mind not to put any stumbling block or obstacle in your brother's way" (Rom. 14:13). Practicing the above principles will help us share our feelings without putting a stumbling block in someone's way.

It sometimes feels that breaking a pattern of negative thinking is as complicated as trying to unscramble an egg. But, in fact, the whole mental process begins with the will—the God-given will—each of us has within.

Victor Frankl was a 26-year-old Jewish psychiatrist in Vienna, Austria, when he was arrested by Hitler's Gestapo and placed in a concentration camp. Month in and month out, he worked beneath the great smokestacks that belched out the black carbon monoxide from the incinerators where his father, mother, sister, and wife had been cremated.

Each day he hoped for the favor of a line-server who would dip down into the broth a little deeper to come up with a few slivers of carrots or peas in the daily bowl of soup. The soup, plus a piece of black bread, made up the monotonous daily menu. In cold weather he got up an hour earlier than usual to use the burlap and wire he had scrounged to wrap his feet and legs against the crippling cold of an eastern European winter. His good shoes and warm socks had long since been appropriated by the guards.

When Frankl was finally called for interrogation, he stood naked in the center of a well-defined circle illuminated on the concrete by a powerful, white light. Men in shiny boots strode noisily in the darkened shadows beyond the light.

For hours the questions and accusations were shot at him by strident voices. They tried to break him down with every accusing lie they could conjure. Already they had taken his journal, his clothes, his wedding ring, and everything else of material value. In the midst of this barrage of questions, an idea flashed across this young Jew's mind. He said to himself, *They have taken from me everything I have except the power to choose my own attitude.*

We have the same power. If we are critical toward others, we can change our negative thinking. If we are the object of criticism, we can choose to overcome it by choosing a positive attitude.

1. "The Apocrypha is a group of religious books not included in the Protestant Bible. These books were written by Christian and Jewish writers. Some Jews thought the books should be included in the Bible. The Roman Catholic Bible includes some of the Apocrypha." [Albert Truesdale, et al., *A Dictionary of the Bible and Christian Doctrine* (Kansas City: Beacon Hill Press of Kansas City, 1986), 28.]

2. "A High Germanic language usually written in Hebrew characters that is spoken by Jews chiefly in eastern Europe." [*Webster's New Collegiate Dictionary,* 9th ed., s.v. "Yiddish."]

Background Scripture: Isa. 6:1-8; James 3:4-6; Matt. 7:1-2

Les Parrott III is a professor of psychology at Seattle Pacific University, a medical psychologist at the University of Washington, and an ordained Nazarene minister.

▼▼▼

A Quick Look Ahead

- There are several common mistakes we make when friends come to us for help: We give them advice. We say, "I understand." We tell them about our similar situations. We dismiss them with an "I'll be praying for you." We say only, "Jesus is the answer."

- The first step in helping is to be available, to give our physical presence and full attention.

- The critical component in helping is listening. Effective listening involves interacting with people in a way that shows respect for their feelings.

- Not until we have listened to our friends will we have earned the right to be part of the third step: the process of solution. We must respect them enough to allow them to work through their own problems.

- Once a person has thought about what has worked in the past and considered various options, he or she needs to decide on a course of action.

9

How to Help a Friend

by Cynthia V. MacDonald

IT HAPPENED AGAIN in my adult Sunday School class. As we discussed a certain Bible passage, I confessed my frustration. I admitted that I was failing in my attempt to apply this scripture to a particularly difficult struggle in my life.

The reaction from the group was typical: advice—and lots of it. I could almost envision a circle of fingers being shaken at me. But I didn't need advice, at least not yet. What I really needed was someone to help me sort through several confusing options.

Offering the right kind of help is one of the most blessed gifts we can give. I believe that much of what we consider helping, however, is ineffective. Even Christians—perhaps *especially* Christians—fail to offer this essential gift because, although we want to be compassionate, we really don't know how. And helping is hard—we make mistakes.

Mistakes We Make

There are several common mistakes we make when friends come to us for help:

We give them advice. This can communicate the insulting implication that they cannot figure out what to do themselves. It may also be arrogant to suggest that we know more about their situation than they do.

We say, "I understand." This can be deadly to hurting people. It's likely that we cannot understand fully. No situation we have experienced is exactly like theirs. Their feelings and reactions are unique.

We tell them about our similar situations. All of a sudden the conversation is about *us* and not them, and they feel ignored and frustrated.

We dismiss them with an "I'll be praying for you." Certainly we should pray, but that shouldn't be the extent of the help we offer.

We say only, "Jesus is the answer." They either know this already and need more than a reminder, or they don't know it and the phrase means nothing to them. Jesus *is* the answer, but He may want to use *us* as His means to deliver it.

What, then, is the right way to help a hurting friend?

Be Available

The first step in helping is to be available, to give our physical presence and full attention. Jesus continually made himself available to people—as He traveled, as He taught, even when He had planned a retreat for the disciples. He spent time with His grieving disciples in an upper room after the Crucifixion, greeting them with "Peace be with you" (Luke 24:36). He appeared to the men on the way to Emmaus and walked with them for a while (vv. 13-16).

Job's friends were available. They quickly and compassionately rallied around him in his pain. For seven days, they suffered in silence with him. But after a week, they began to fail him. They refused to accept Job's claim that he had been faithful to God. Instead, they insisted that he must have sinned, and they tried to impose solutions to his dilemma. "Should God then reward you on your terms, when you refuse to repent?" Elihu said (34:33). "Curse God and die!" Job's wife suggested (2:9).

We, too, run the danger of offering bad advice when we move directly from being available to discussing a plan of action. There is an important step in between.

Listen Effectively

The critical component in helping is *listening*. Effective listening involves interacting with people in a way that shows respect for their feelings. Even if our intentions are good, immediately jumping in with solutions—thus ignoring what they say—shows a lack of respect.

Reflect the content. The first step in listening is to reflect the content of what a person says—using different words to repeat what he or she communicated. This process may seem awkward or phony at first, but it will sound more strange to us than to the person we are helping. This skill has two important benefits: (1) It forces us to pay close attention, and (2) it tells the other person that we have heard him or her.

At times, Jesus reflected to people what He heard them say. After a short exchange, Nathanael declared Jesus to be the Son of God. Jesus reflected back to him the basis of his faith: "You believe because I told you I saw you under the fig tree" (John 1:50).

When I commented about my difficulty with the Bible passage, the others in my Sunday School class could have said, "It is hard to apply this verse to our lives." Then I would have known that they had really heard my complaint, and that they empathized with what is surely a common plight.

Clarify the hidden need. Reflecting the message works best when we reflect not only the content but also the emotion and need behind what is said. The harried Martha complained to Jesus, "Lord, don't you care that my sister has left me to do the work by myself? Tell her to help me!" (Luke 10:40). Before offering a solution, Jesus reflected back to her the heart of her problem, which went much deeper than household help: "You are worried and upset about many things" (v. 41).

We, too, can minister to people by reflecting their feelings and clarifying the needs they express. As a public high school teacher, I sometimes come home with a litany of discouraging events. My husband, Roy, used to respond with, "Cheer up!" Or, "You should count your blessings." Or even, "Uh huh." Now, however, he says, "You sound discouraged." Or, "You must have had a hard day." Or, "You need a hug." I much prefer the new Roy. Now I feel as if he really listens to me—not only to what I say but to what I need.

We must be careful not to overanalyze, though, when we reflect people's feelings. We should reflect just the obvious feelings: "That must have hurt your feelings," or "You sound angry." We shouldn't try to interpret and suggest, for example, that they must be acting out a childhood trauma. Such a statement would be a wild guess and could even be harmful.

Reflect the confusion. Reflective listening is probably most helpful when persons have confused or ambivalent feelings. If we can repeat what they say, they can recognize their confusion and take constructive action. Jesus did this when the father of a son possessed by an evil spirit said to Him, "If you can do anything, take pity on us and help us" (Mark 9:22). Jesus repeated his words in the form of a question, "If you can?" (v. 23), and clarified the man's ambivalence about his faith. Then He said, "Everything is possible for him who believes" (v. 23), allowing him the opportunity to decide on a clear path of action. The man decided: "I do believe; help me overcome my unbelief!" (v. 24).

Search for Solutions

How, then, do we help people arrive at solutions? Not until we have listened to our friends will we have earned the right to be part of the third step: the process of solution. We must respect them enough to allow them to solve their own problems. Our main goal should be to encourage people to find their own solutions. We can help this process along by asking questions.

Talk about the present. People searching for solutions to a problem first need to talk about the present situation. Sometimes a simple fact-finding question reveals a lot. Jesus asked a demoniac, "What is your name?" The astounding answer, "Legion" (Mark 5:9), was more than an interesting tidbit—it was a revelation of the man's whole problem. He was possessed by a multitude of evil spirits. No wonder his behavior was destructive.

Focus on what they are requesting. Next, help hurting persons define exactly what needs to be done. Jesus asked blind Bartimaeus, "What do you want me to do for you?" (Mark 10:51). Surely He knew, but He wanted Bartimaeus to articulate his need. Understanding what the problem is can be an important step in healing.

Help generate alternatives. Encourage them to come up with their own solutions. Avoid the temptation to offer ours. Ask them to consider the past, to remember what has worked before to solve a problem. When the disciples were worried about not having enough bread, Jesus used a series of questions to remind them of the miraculous way in which He had just fed the multitudes (Mark 8:14-21). They needed to remember and understand that Jesus was the solution to their problem.

Offer suggestions. If a friend truly cannot come up with a practical course of action, we may—carefully—suggest one, but only after all the steps previously mentioned have been exhausted. And get permission first. Ask, "Would you like to know what worked for me?" or "for a friend?" or "in the Bible?"

Commit to Action

Finally, once a person has thought about what has worked in the past and considered various options, he or she needs to decide on a course of action.

Jesus helped a Samaritan woman at the well to move from a position of pain and rejection to a position of acting in hope and faith (John 4:1-26). She was confused about the issue of where to worship God—on the mountain or in Jerusalem. Jesus understood her desire to know God, summarized the two options she had articulated, and offered a third, couched in nonthreatening terms, as one that "true worshipers" were choosing: worshiping God "in spirit and truth" (v. 23). Then she offered her own solution, "When [Messiah] comes, he will explain everything to us" (v. 25). She had committed to an action—pursuit of faith—so she was ready for Jesus' revelation, "I who speak to you am he" (v. 26).

We can help friends reach the stage of action by continuing to serve as a sounding board. Rephrase their ideas as they move toward a solution, and help them to clarify their needs and options. Then, once we have found out what they really want to do, encourage them to do it.

Jesus was encouraging people to action when He said

to the rich young ruler, who was apparently seeking more fulfillment, "Follow me" (Mark 10:21). To the nobleman with the paralyzed servant, "Go! It will be done just as you believed it would" (Matt. 8:13). To the woman caught in adultery, "Go now and leave your life of sin" (John 8:11). And to the disciples, "Go into all the world and preach the good news to all creation" (Mark 16:15).

We, too, can encourage people to follow a course of action. But we need to be sure that the course of action comes from God to them—and not from us.

We can, through listening, help our friends. What a wonderful gift to give!

Background Scripture: Mark 10:46-52; Luke 10:38-42; 24:13-16; John 8:1-11

Cynthia V. MacDonald teaches English at Libertyville High School in Libertyville, Ill.

▼▼▼

A Quick Look Ahead

- Parents are often faced with a child doing wrong. Cheating on exams, skipping classes, or refusing to do responsible tasks at home are just some of the behaviors. But increasing numbers of kids are involved in more serious actions—like drug and alcohol abuse, theft, sexual promiscuity, and violence.

- The first message a hurting family needs to hear is assurance that others care and are not condemning them. Churches need to pray and work to create an atmosphere in which Christian nurture can thrive.

- There are four basic reasons why young people engage in misbehavior: They rebel against boundaries they consider to be rigid and unrealistic. Teenagers test the limits of inconsistent or permissive parents. Juveniles act out the pain of adjusting to those circumstances over which they have no control. They get involved in antisocial behavior to gain acceptance from a peer group.

10

When Kids Get in Trouble

by Grace Ketterman

"HOW COULD YOU do this to us?" Janet* screamed at her 16-year-old daughter. Michelle* had just revealed in their family doctor's office that she was pregnant.

It was a moment of anguish for both mother and daughter. Janet and her husband had tried hard to be good parents. They attended church faithfully, tried to live their beliefs, and taught their children about living the Christian life. Yet, Michelle's sexual behavior and unplanned pregnancy seemed proof that they had failed. How could they face their friends—or their pastor?

What Michelle had "done to" her parents was not an act against them. Michelle loved her parents and was horrified about the impact of her actions. She would have given anything to undo the last three months. Yet she knew many of her friends, even in her youth group, had engaged in the same behaviors. They just hadn't gotten caught.

Twenty-four painful hours later, Michelle and her parents met with their pastor. He listened supportively as each family member verbalized pain, anger, and confusion. He guided them in understanding Michelle's relationship with Kent*, her boyfriend. He reminded the parents that our children do not always do what is best for all concerned, but we love them anyway—just as God loves us.

Gradually, Janet and Mike*, her husband, stopped blaming themselves. Perhaps they had given their daughter more freedom than she could handle, but they had allowed their own activities to take away the time they used to spend seeing that her needs were filled. They realized that they had taught her the right values and that she had lived responsibly, except in the area of sexual intimacy.

The following weeks seemed like an eternity of searching for alternatives to abortion. Michelle wished that she and Kent would get married and make a home for this baby. Kent and his family, meanwhile, suffered through their own anger and blame. Eventually, the two families pulled together and helped the teenagers find answers. They located a couple who would adopt and give the baby the care they could not.

What Happened?

This is a common problem: Parents are often faced with a child doing wrong. Cheating on exams, skipping classes, or refusing to do responsible tasks at home are just some of the behaviors. But increasing numbers of kids are involved in more serious actions—like drug and alcohol abuse, theft, sexual promiscuity, and violence.

Whatever the offense, parents face five major challenges:

1. They must gain perspective on their own emotions and regain a measure of composure. Feelings that are intense tend to cloud wise or calm thinking.

2. To help their troubled child, they need to find ways to restore open and loving communication. Often parents are unaware of the barriers that have been steadily building and stifling communication.

3. The entire family needs to be involved in finding solutions for the problem that has been revealed. Permanent answers will not occur if parents "fix" whatever was done wrong. Long-lasting behavior changes are found when the "offender" is part of developing the solution.

4. After the first three steps are successfully operating, the family is better prepared to deal with reactions coming from outside the family.

5. No particular step-by-step approach to a crisis has any guarantee of working every time for every family. Whether the procedures mentioned above reestablish open communication or whether other problems surface and communication breaks down, families can be open to forgiveness and the work of God's redemptive grace.

The Role of the Church

Certainly, a most significant work of the church is to be a body encouraging repentance, restitution, and restoration. In some notable situations this has not been done. In one church, a young person had committed a sin that shocked and hurt a number of other people. Though he repented with intense remorse, the membership shunned him. His parents were no longer considered for church offices, and the entire family eventually left the church.

To avoid a similar scenario, here are some possible actions a healthy, Spirit-led church could take:

● There should be teaching in sermons, adult classes, and seminars that focuses on acceptance and restoration. This is vividly depicted in the parable of the lost son (Luke 15:32).

● Small groups should be formed to provide support for families struggling with similar problems.

● The church should be intentional about strengthening children and youth ministries to provide positive environments for children.

● People graced in forgiveness and helping wounded members should be paired with hurting families. Many Christians would like to reach out in a difficult situation, but they do not know how. Compassionate training could teach them how to help appropriately.

Here are some helpful ways to approach wounded families.

● "I know you are having a difficult time right now. I want you to know I care. I'd like to go to the court date with you. What time may I pick you up?"

● "Could you come to our house for dinner Sunday?"

● "Our son and daughter are having some friends over for pizza after the game Friday, and we'd like to include your children. Our son or daughter will call to invite your children personally."

● In the face of spreading gossip, simply say to the family, "We've heard about your pain. We don't need any details, but please know we love you. We're here for you."

● Offer to the family, "On Tuesday evening we'd like to take you out for coffee. Just to let you know we're standing by you." Often parents feel shame over a child's problems and may at first refuse such a gesture. Don't let that be a deterrent. Respect their privacy. Accept their refusal, but make the offer again soon.

Repeating such offers of help, while maintaining a genuine attitude of warmth and caring, will reach even the most independent of suffering people.

What Hurting Families Need

The first message a hurting family needs to hear is assurance that others care and are not condemning them.

Recently, I sat in an infant dedication service. How tender and sacred it was! One of the more sobering parts of that event was the challenge to the congregation. After the parents had made their commitment to raise their child according to God's Word, the pastor asked those assembled if they, too, would promise to support and encourage the child and the parents. Solemnly they pledged, "We will."

Truly the church shares responsibility for both the successes and the failures of its youth. Commonly, people frown with disapproval and gossip about the waywardness of an individual. They do not pray, and they rarely reach out in friendship to the hurting one.

Families who have a troubled child need for other young people from the church to befriend that youngster. Yet, most church parents are worried about allowing their children to associate with such a child. They are afraid their "good" kids will be contaminated.

Churches need to pray and work to create an atmosphere in which Christian nurture can thrive. Reaching out to help a weaker brother or sister results in growth. When Christians learn to help a stumbling peer, everyone benefits.

Guidance and support by adult youth leaders and pastoral staff are important. If a teenager, for example, is to befriend a rebellious peer, there should be a carefully selected group that prays regularly for both. The helping teen needs an adult who understands the situation and is trusted by both families to meet with regularly for guidance. The parents of the troubled youth should be a part of the entire process, and their permission is vital before the effort is begun.

Genuine Christian concern and prayerful, loving action will reach the target—the heart of the troubled youth.

Understanding the Straying Teen

There are four basic reasons why young people engage in misbehavior.

They rebel against boundaries they consider to be rigid and unrealistic. Some families are unreasonably strict and unbending. The difficulty is finding the proper balance between freedom and restrictions.

Teens' major developmental tasks are learning how to be successfully independent, how to make wise decisions, and how to face consequences responsibly. When parents make too many decisions for their children, they deny them the chance to learn from experience. This sets the stage for rebellion, especially when parents treat teens as children, or in other ways belittle them.

Teenagers test the limits of inconsistent or permissive parents. Reliable studies clearly show that children function best and develop the healthiest self-esteem when they have clearly defined boundaries. There is one way to prevent either rigidity or the inconsistency of permissiveness. That is to develop gradually expanding boundaries. As a teen shows some responsibility, he or she should be given a proportionate increase in freedom. Teenagers can be a part of establishing family rules and consequences. Doing so greatly reduces the chances of rebellion because they will view as reasonable any boundaries they had a part in creating.

Teenagers act out the pain of adjusting to those circumstances over which they have no control. Many young people live in families filled with anger. They often feel inferior to peers and find few areas of success in their lives. Sometimes anxious, depressed, or angry kids try to feel better by using drugs or by escaping through the excitement of misbehavior.

They get involved in antisocial behavior to gain acceptance from a peer group. Often troubled teens find acceptance from their peers rather than their family. Thus their need to belong is satisfied, and self-confidence grows. The problem, of course, is that troubled teens nearly always find their sense of belonging from equally troubled kids—or worse!

Some Answers from the Church

Understanding the reasons for the rebellion of teens opens up some exciting challenges for the church. Here are some suggestions:

● Review and revise, if necessary, all programs for children and youth. These programs need to focus on a total commitment to the Lordship of Jesus Christ.

● Youth need to understand the dangers of sin and need to be pointed to God's forgiveness and the empowerment of His Spirit to overcome sin.

● Youth need to be challenged to service for Christ. There are needs in our world that youth can fill by reaching out to others who hurt. Many churches have tried entertaining kids instead of challenging them.

● Moms and dads want instruction about successful parenting. Bible-based teaching, support groups, and family-to-family partnerships could be offered to both prevent and heal hurts.

Children need four things from adults for emotional health:

● They need unconditional love. Christ offers that throughout the Gospels. Even 1 Corinthians 13 says love "is not self-seeking, it is not easily angered, it keeps no record of wrongs" (v. 5).

● They need predictability. Being consistent is not easy. Often we react according to our feelings instead of following a logical plan.

● They need approval. To feel they have worth is not easy for average kids. For example, it's easy for ordinary kids to feel lost in huge schools. The church can give them a place to feel like they belong.

● They need to know the "cheerful heart" as described in Prov. 17:22 as "good medicine." Life becomes serious, painful, almost unbearable at times. A healthy sense of humor sometimes helps in balancing life.

Life isn't easy for teenagers or adults. But through the help of Jesus Christ we can lay a good foundation and overcome every difficulty.

*Name has been changed.

Background Scripture: 2 Cor. 1:3-7; Gal. 6:2; Rom. 12:15

Grace Ketterman is a Kansas City counselor who works with troubled children.

▼▼▼

A Quick Look Ahead

- When someone does not share in what defines the group, it is easy to feel out of sync. One's self-esteem can suffer under such conditions. Often the group unintentionally weakens a person's self-esteem by emphasizing what the members have in common and widening the gap.

- For childless couples, the spiritual impulse is to ask *why*— Why us? Why now? Why this? Their spiritual self-esteem falters. They question whether God loves them as much as He loves those who have children. They wonder if they are being punished for something they have done. They fear that God has deemed them unsuitable for parenthood. They often feel like they don't fit in.

- As Christians, we should be inclusive in our churches, rather than exclusive. Our task is to bring the healing of the gospel to those who hurt, not to isolate certain persons from our midst because they do not fit in.

11

When I Don't Fit In

by Gay L. Leonard

LIKE IT OR NOT, we have certain working definitions in every group. These definitions, or "norms," may be largely unspoken, but they exist and control how persons are allowed to fit in to the group. There are certain ways persons are expected to be or to act in order to feel accepted.

For example, any Sunday School class can be defined by the characteristics that fit the majority of its members. Traits like what kinds of jobs they have—blue collar or professional. Whether they are shy and retiring or outgoing and fun-loving. Whether they are newly married or celebrating "golden" anniversaries, or even married or single, including all categories of singleness—never married, divorced, widowed. And whether they have children or grandchildren.

When someone does not share in what defines the group, it is easy to feel out of sync. One's self-esteem can suffer under such conditions. Often the group unintentionally weakens a person's self-esteem by emphasizing what the members have in common and widening the gap. The class members naturally spend a great deal of time talking together about what is happening (that is, about what is important to them) in their lives. Those who do not have similar events to discuss can feel left out. Being left out can be a painful experience.

This chapter is going to discuss what it feels like to be out of sync emotionally. We could concentrate on how it feels to be shy. Or we could explore the feelings of divorced, widowed, or never-married persons. However, we are going to specifically consider the pain suffered by childless couples. The principles we will discuss in this area apply to all persons who do not feel they fit in the group. Please keep other categories in mind as this chapter is read. Think about how divorced people feel in a class full of married couples. Or how widowed people perceive a group of retired couples. Or how single parents hear married parents talk about the struggles of their lives. Or how shy persons react to a class full of outgoing, laughing people.

Please try to keep all those persons in mind as we hear about a specific agony—infertility.

A Wedge Between Friends

Pam and Donna were the best of friends. They enjoyed similar office careers, attended the same Sunday School class, and socialized on weekends. To their happy surprise, they both became pregnant about the same time.

As Donna anticipated a sibling playmate for her daughter, Pam dreamed of holding her own baby. They shared their anticipation and joy, shopped for baby supplies together, and planned on seeing each other through the delivery.

But Pam's dreams were shattered one day when she was rushed to the hospital in intense pain. Testing determined that the embryo had implanted in the wall of a tube rather than in the uterus. She was whisked off to surgery where she lost not only the baby but also one tube and an ovary. Doctors told her that her chances of conceiving again were now less than 50 percent.

While Donna blossomed through her pregnancy, Pam languished in grief. Repeated attempts to become pregnant failed. With each passing month Pam slipped deeper into despair. When Donna gave birth to a healthy son, Pam could not share in the joy. The relationship became too painful, and finally she told Donna that their friendship would have to end.

Donna was hurt and bewildered. Pam, in her anguish, was repulsed by her own feelings of irrepressible jealousy. She had lost more than a baby. She had lost a friend.

Infertility Is Widespread

While devastating, Pam's situation is by no means unique. Experts estimate that 1 in 12 couples is infertile. This includes those who have long-term difficulty conceiving, as well as those who can never conceive. Others believe this number is actually much higher, since many couples never disclose their fertility difficulties to anyone.

Infertility is constantly in the news—from medical breakthroughs to talk shows to courtroom dramas. Why this sudden "epidemic" of infertility? While many have speculated about substances in the water or environmental pollution, the truth of the matter is that the percentage of couples within each age-group unable to conceive has remained constant for decades. We are hearing more about infertility today because society allows public communication about private matters, and fertility advances are encouraging couples to speak openly and seek treatment.

In addition, the choice among some women to not have children until a later age has increased their chances of experiencing infertility. Consequently, doctors are seeing more cases of infertility than ever before.

What are the chances of being among the millions of infertile couples? The National Center for Health Statistics reports that between the ages of 15 and 24 years, 4.1 percent of all women are infertile. Between 25 and 34 years of age, the percentage increases to 13.4 percent, and from 35 to 44 years, the percentage jumps to 21.4 percent. What do these numbers mean to us? Some couple we know in our church—perhaps even in our Sunday School class—may be experiencing this situation, and it is likely that they have not "gone public" with their very private pain.

Because their lives differ in many respects from their child-bearing counterparts, infertile couples may feel out of sync with the rest of society. Since they are afraid to disclose their infertility problems, they learn to tolerate a variety of questions and ill-informed observations: "What you need to settle you down is two or three little ones." "When are you planning to have children?" "You wouldn't understand. You're not a parent."

Because they feel their childlessness separates them from the rest of society, they question their acceptance on a variety of levels.

For those couples, the spiritual impulse is to ask *why*—Why us? Why now? Why this? Their spiritual self-esteem falters. They question whether God loves them as much as He does those who have children. They wonder if they are being punished for something they have done. They fear that God has deemed them unsuitable for parenthood. They often feel like they don't fit in.

How Does Infertility Feel?

"Father's Day," a story by Roxie Martin, describes the emotional agony firsthand. Here is a portion of her story:

He was used to the crying by now.

Oh, at first it had bothered him a lot. In fact, that

first morning, he had jumped out of bed and rushed to her side. He couldn't remember exactly how it went, but he was sure he put his arms around her and kissed her and whispered all the right words—cheery, hopeful, baby-talking words.

The monthly ritual was beginning to tire him now. Nor did Keri have the heart for it anymore. She used to cry "regular" tears, with just a few wails in between. Then she would reach for his comforting arms gratefully. Now she sobbed her bitter anger at God behind the slammed bathroom door.

With the last sniffle, Keri returned to the bedroom and began pulling on her church clothes. "Happy Father's Day, Jack," she said, flatly.

WHUMP! The words hit him like a fastball to the chest. When he could breathe again, he sat up. "Stop it, Keri. Stop it! You've got to let go. Maybe we were never meant to have a baby. We've just got to get on with our lives. Together, I hope." He knew those weren't the right words. He hadn't quite said it the way he felt it; but that was quite a speech, for Jack.

In response, Keri retreated to the bathroom to finish getting ready for church. Jack wanted to cry too. Not for the Baby with a capital "B," but for Keri. The real Keri who wasn't cold and dried-up with disappointment. The Keri that he loved—and missed. He crawled out of bed, feeling elderly.

The adult Sunday School they attended was famous for "gabbing" before the lesson. This Sunday they were talking even longer. Sandy, the teacher's wife, was finishing up plans for an evening fellowship.

"Let's get a count now," Sandy said. "How many kids will need church child-care Friday night? Whites, two; Larkins, one; Jeffers, three; Meyers—hey, you two need to get with it. We're about to run out of babies in this class!"

Jack couldn't make his mouth work, but Keri smiled her cutest smile and said, "What? And end our 10-year honeymoon?" Her comeback delighted everyone. Except Jack. He wasn't laughing. He knew exactly how much those quick responses cost her.

These people are our friends. We've known them for years. But when it comes to what's really on our hearts, they might as well be strangers.

Jack sat through the lesson numbly, avoiding Keri's pasted-on smile. He was vaguely aware that the lesson was about fathers. He caught the phrases "family shepherd" and "spiritual leader." He heard someone mention something about strength.

Jack realized too late that he was being addressed. "Well . . . ," he said, stalling for an answer. Then, he heard himself confess, "Ron, I apologize. I wasn't listening. To be honest, I was sitting here feeling sorry for myself because I'm not a father, and probably never will be. Keri and I have tried everything we've ever heard or read about, every doctor who would see us, and still no baby. I don't have the slightest idea of what it means to be the 'spiritual head' of a family that includes children. I guess the lesson's not for me today."

The adult Sunday School class stopped cold. For a long moment no one spoke. Keri's fingernails dug into Jack's arm. He couldn't look at her. He knew she was furious.

"I'm sorry," Jack continued. "I shouldn't have dropped that on you here. This isn't really the time or place. Please, go on with the lesson."

He was interrupted by a chorus of protest: "We didn't have any idea." "I'm so sorry." "We've been so insensitive."

Sandy was the most embarrassed. "Why didn't you stop me?"

Ron's voice restored order. "No, Jack, we're sorry. I'm ashamed that our class is a place where people feel like they have to hide their hurts. I wish I could tell you why things haven't worked out for you, but I can't. All I can tell you is that whether or not He sends you a baby, He can heal our hearts. Can we pray for forgiveness for our insensitivity? And pray with you in your hurt? Jack? Keri?"

Jack looked at Keri, whose gaze was concentrated on a single pleat in her skirt. She nodded her head a fraction of an inch. "Yes," Jack said. "Please."

And that's how Jack and Keri came to be permanent fixtures on the adult Sunday School class's prayer list. In fact, that's what started the idea of replacing the prelesson gabbing with a time of silent prayer. As they arrive, the members write a prayer concern on the chalkboard and join the group. And that's how the adult Sunday School class came to be known as "the prayer meetin' class."

Emotional Agony

As the above story shows, infertile couples face a myriad of emotions and spiritual questions they can neither explain nor seem to escape. While women are more likely to express themselves, men also experience these symptoms of emotional upheaval:

- **Hostility.** At one time or another, the emptiness expresses itself in anger. Sometimes the target is a pregnant woman, a new parent, some well-meaning person who gives unwanted advice at an inopportune moment, or even God. They may be angry about the expense and indignity of infertility treatments. Often infertility is accompanied by marital problems, as spouses lash out at each other in tension and stress.

- **Jealousy.** Like Pam, they have intense jealousy of other couples who are able to conceive and bear children—what some have termed the profound ache of "baby lust."
- **Fear.** Childless couples fear people feeling sorry for them. They fear being excluded from certain segments of society and becoming self-centered. They fear growing old alone, without any family.
- **Grief.** With any loss comes grief. Whether it be the baby lost in miscarriage or the baby lost by never having conceived at all, sooner or later most infertile couples will face the grieving process with all of its phases—denial, anger, sorrow, and acceptance.
- **Guilt.** Infertile couples also suffer a false sense of guilt. Traditionally, the woman has been blamed for fertility problems. In the biblical accounts of infertility, Sarah, Rachel, and Hannah—not their husbands—bear the stigma. Throughout history and across many cultures, childless women have been shunned. King Henry VIII discarded one wife after another as each failed to give him an heir. Only a century ago, a barren woman was presumed to have been sexually promiscuous.

Couples Are Infertile

Today, the cause of infertility is often medically pinpointed as the problem of husband *or* wife. While the cause of some cases still remains a mystery, about 40 percent of the time a couple's lack of conception can be explained by some problem in the woman's reproductive system. Another 40 percent of infertility cases are traced to the man. The remaining 20 percent result from subtle deviations in each partner that together create an infertile situation.

This ability of the medical profession to isolate the "infertile partner" has produced a whole new set of issues for childless couples. In fact, I heard one spouse say in public that she "forgave" her husband for their not being able to have children. This "forgiveness" implied guilt and blame. The terrible anguish of infertility sometimes looks for a target—someone or something upon which to vent anger and frustration. Isolating the responsible party has divided some childless couples to the point of divorce.

In reality, there are no infertile *partners;* there are only infertile *couples.* Struggles must be faced together, with partners gaining strength from one another.

How Should the Church Respond?

As Christians, we should be inclusive in our churches, rather than exclusive. Our task is to bring the healing of the gospel to those who hurt, not to isolate certain persons from our midst because they do not fit in.

How can the church do this?

Recognizing the tremendous emotional and spiritual upheaval when a person feels out of sync, the church can take specific steps to show its support:

● **Be sensitive to needs and feelings.** Consciously work to make everyone feel fully accepted in every activity and ministry of the church. Be especially understanding on holidays, particularly Mother's Day and Father's Day—two of the most painful days of the year for childless, unmarried, grieving, or widowed persons in the congregation.

• **Talk openly and show genuine care.** Find out what
people need. And make every effort to find ways for them
to fill those needs.

• **Guard against careless remarks and criticism.** The
very behavior others dislike in a childless couple, a never-
married person, a single parent, or a widowed individual
may be their emotional cover-up. Be understanding of
their behavior. Careless words can sting like salt in a fresh-
ly opened wound.

• **Make every effort to become the Christian friend**
or part of a circle of friends with whom persons feeling out
of sync can openly share emotional struggles and find encouragement.

Actually, we all may be out of sync in some way with
others in the church. Try to create a nurturing environment
that will break down barriers and help all persons to feel
they are loved and accepted.

No one understands why life is so painful for some,
but we do know that God wants to wrap everyone in His
love. Someone we know is the "1 in 12" who is infertile,
the never-married person, the single parent, or the widowed individual. Someone we don't know well enough is
the shy person sitting quietly in class. We should be about
the business of better understanding, supporting, and loving them.

We should create an atmosphere of love and acceptance that will allow all persons in the church to find it unnecessary to say, "I don't fit in."

Background Scripture: Gen. 29:32; 30:1-2; 1 Sam. 1:1-8

Gay L. Leonard is a pastor's wife, freelance writer, and speaker who lives in Or-
lando, Fla.

A Quick Look Ahead

- "People are not *things* to be manipulated with the right techniques," I said. "They are not creatures to be *used* to further our own economic self-interest. People are sacred! Each of them is an infinitely precious person . . . and all of them deserve to be treated with reverent respect."

- Lack of fulfillment and the absence of "fun" on the job are responsible for more evil than can be measured. At their worst, people's attempts to allay the feelings of deadness that result from unfulfilling work can include adultery, wife-beating, and brutalizing children.

- A mission statement is the setting down in clear and specific words the purposes and goals of life. It is a statement of what we feel will make our life successful in following God's plan.

▲▲▲

12

Developing a Christian View of Success*

by Tony Campolo

THE EXECUTIVES of a large insurance corporation had brought in an array of top-flight speakers to teach their sales force the most successful techniques for marketing their product. The audience listened with riveted attention as a number of experts in behavioral psychology explained how to "set up" clients, push the right emotional buttons, and close the deal. The presentations were brilliant!

It was my task to end with a motivational talk that would "psych up" the sales teams to get the job done. You can imagine the surprise, then, that greeted my opening words: "Everything you've heard today is wrong."

Disbelief flooded the faces of the company's executives, and as I surveyed the crowd, I knew I had their attention.

"People are not *things* to be manipulated with the right techniques," I said. "They are not creatures to be *used* to further our own economic self-interest. People are sacred! Each of them is an infinitely precious person in whom the Eternal God has chosen to make His home. And all of them deserve to be treated with reverent respect.

"You don't have to manipulate people if you're selling something they really need," I said. "All you have to do is show them the seriousness of their need and then demonstrate how what you have to offer can meet that need.

"You're selling life insurance!" I declared. "That's something people really *do* need for the security of their families. Recognize that! You lower yourself if you take a noble profession like selling insurance that people need, and turn it into the work of a con artist."

When I finished, the crowd was on its feet cheering, and the president of the company was leading the applause. He wanted his sales staff to be more than money-grubbers. He wanted them to be proud of themselves and what they did to make a living.

And don't we all want to feel that way? The good news is: There is an alternative to the view of the marketplace as a jungle where only the strong and the shrewd survive.

I'm thoroughly convinced that something fantastic can happen when the affairs of a business and the relationships of people in the workaday world are guided by the hand of God instead of by the invisible hand of iron-fisted economics, which makes profit the bottom line and erodes the self-respect of workers who feel they must be dishonest to succeed. No wonder people hate their jobs!

God has something better in mind. To discover it, we must set aside society's version of success and focus, instead, on the biblical view.

How Can I Feel Good About Myself if I Dislike My Job?

Whenever I counsel people whose primary problem in life is tied up with job dissatisfaction, I ask them if they have ever dreamed of doing something different. In almost every case, these people's faces light up as they describe the glorious plans they have hatched in their minds. But they do not carry out their plans because they cannot bring themselves to risk their limited security.

That's a tragedy, because job satisfaction is crucial for the success of family life. A spouse who spends eight hours a day in a job that is emotionally draining and unfulfilling is a spouse who may have a low libido and be a lousy lover. Countless divorces can be traced to vocational activities that left people dehumanized and emotionally dead.

Any survey of workers in business and industry will reveal that a large number suffer regular bouts of depression. These workers, in interviews with researchers, make statements such as the following:

"I am really a nobody."

"Nothing I do really matters."

"I get treated like dirt at work."

"I have no fun at what I do all day."

Lack of fulfillment and the absence of fun on the job are responsible for more evil than can be measured. At their worst, people's attempts to allay the feelings of deadness that result from unfulfilling work can include adultery, wife-beating, and brutalizing children. Sometimes these dissatisfied people work little, yet come home exhausted. Their exhaustion comes not from physical exertion but from a sense of meaninglessness and an absence of fulfillment of their creative powers.

This problem affects all age-groups. Recently, while interacting with a group of university students, I found myself increasingly frustrated as they talked about their lack of enthusiasm for life. They seemed bored with themselves and disinterested in anyone else. Finally, in exasperation I shouted, "I'm 57 and you're 21, and I am younger than you are because people are as young as their dreams and as old as their cynicism. And you've got no dreams or visions."

Visions are what energize and drive us. Dreams lift us out of the doldrums and give a lilt to our step. With God's help we can determine our own dreams and visions. The prophet Isaiah says: "But those who hope in the Lord will renew their strength. They will soar on wings like eagles; they will run and not grow weary, they will walk and not be faint" (Isa. 40:31).

The solution to the work-related depression that permeates our society is not to be found in the world's cockeyed view of success. If we want our work to be of lasting significance, we should consider establishing a "mission statement" for our lives.

How to Identify Our Purposes and Goals

A mission statement is the setting down in clear and specific words the purposes and goals of life. It is a statement of what we feel will make our life successful in following God's plan. And if it's an honest and good mission statement, it can *generate such energy that even the young will be amazed.*

When I was 40 years old, I went through a kind of mini identity crisis. I had been teaching sociology on the university level for more than 15 years, and I wasn't sure I wanted to *be* a sociologist for the rest of my life.

At one point, my craving for significance drove me into politics. It was a kind of spur-of-the-moment decision based on the commonly accepted premise of the time that politicians are the ones who can make the greatest impact on the world.

In 1976 I entered the race for a seat in the U.S. Congress from the Fifth District of Pennsylvania. I won the primary but was soundly defeated in the general election.

As I look back, I can honestly say I'm glad I didn't win. If I had won, I might have been trapped in a life-track that would have kept me from what has given me a much fuller sense of joyful purpose.

Shortly after the campaign was over, three very close friends I had been having a weekly Bible study with agreed to get with me and help me think through and pray through what my life should be about. Since it was obvious that a life in politics was not going to be my future, we thought it would be a good idea to try to figure out just what I should do and be.

Our discussions led to an all-day get-together in which we hammered out some conclusions. It proved to be one of the most important days of my life, because it was the day I was able to specify clearly what I thought would give my life meaning.

First, my friends forced me to set down on paper just what I had been doing up to that point that had been "fun." I know that "fun" sounds terribly unholy, but my friends and I are convinced that God has so designed us that what He has willed for us to do with our lives creates a sense of joy. Upon reflection, I realized that I got my greatest kicks out of talking to college students.

Second, my friends helped me zero in on the primary and most significant thing that I had accomplished through my speaking to college students. I had been able to get a number of them to reconsider their vocational choices. I felt the most right about myself when I could get students to consider how their lives could be invested most effectively to impact others for Christ. I got my greatest high from helping collegians get a vision of the great work that they could do to further the kingdom of God.

Craig, the friend who has always pushed me hardest to define the direction of my life, would not let it rest there.

"Be more specific," he insisted. "Exactly *what* do you want these colleges kids to do with themselves?"

Immediately, it came to me. "I want them to become missionaries!" I blurted. "That's what I want. I want them to become missionaries!"

But Craig didn't leave it at that. "How many of them would have to go to the mission field to leave you with a sense that you had done what you were supposed to do with your life?" A specific number came to mind: 200.

By the end of that afternoon, I had written out my mission for life, and I believe it came from God. It reads: "Before I hang up my sneakers at the end, I want to have motivated and helped at least 200 college and university students to commit themselves to go out as full-time missionaries for the cause of Christ."

Once my mission statement was developed, I had to face the fact that I needed to consider how living out that statement would affect the rest of my life. Obviously, some time would have to be taken away from my wife and children. I would have to think through this conflict of interests and strike up a proper balance. I would have to determine in advance just how much time I would need to give to be the father and husband I should be. This was not simply a matter of determining what I *wanted* to do. It was a matter of what I *ought* to do. My family has been my major source of emotional gratification. I would be sad in the depths of my being if I failed to have the relationships with them that I needed to.

There were other considerations. Relatives, friends, neighbors, students, and colleagues all required time. I had to give careful attention constantly to ensure that my priorities were reflected in my use of time and that, in the midst of living out my obligations to others, my mission in life did not get lost.

Peace Comes in Definition of Purpose

Over the years, I have continued to define myself in terms of my mission rather than in terms of my job. I still teach sociology, but I do not define myself as a sociologist. Sociology is something I *do*. It is not who I *am*.

Who I *am* is a person committed to challenging college students to become missionaries. Right now I think I can best carry out that mission by teaching sociology at a Christian college. However, if I should lose my position, I do not think I would lose my identity. My identity is defined by my mission, and my mission will remain constant regardless of what job changes I make or what roles I may be led to play.

Working out a mission requires time. Even the Son of God had to spend time in private prayer and reflection before fulfilling His messianic role. That is what the 40 days in the wilderness were really all about. It is important to block off sufficient time for such a crucial task. A week of restful introspection would be ideal, but if that is impossible, at least take a weekend.

Second, it is essential to get into the right state of mind. We must become centered on God.

Being still—I mean *really* still—is for me the best spiritual exercise. Being still is more than what comes from the cessation of noise. It is something that goes on inside. It happens when I let my mind quiet down.

If I sit still with my eyes closed and just think of the name of Jesus, if I say His name repeatedly and lovingly, if I submit to the calming feeling that seems to flow into my life as my mind becomes fixed on Him, if I emotionally surrender to a sense of His presence, *then* stillness overtakes me. My mind stops bouncing around like a Ping-Pong ball and, in the quietude that follows, I can sense that "still small voice" (1 Kings 19:12, KJV) at the ground of my being. And I know I am in touch with Him.

I have a friend who gets tuned in to the Spirit by reading from (or perhaps I should say *praying through*) the Book of Psalms. He treats each psalm as a prayer that the writer wrote to express his feelings to God and to verbalize what he really wants from God. "The Psalms," he says, "enable me to ask of God His most precious gift—himself. Through the Psalms I find the words to pray for nothing except that He be with me and in me."

I recently talked to an elderly woman who finds that in reciting the words of favorite hymns her mind becomes open to the voice of God.

Try any of the above. Try all of them. Try none of them and come up with a special way. In the end, a special kind of listening will be learned that nobody need teach. Indeed, nobody *can* teach us. This is the work of the Holy Spirit. Trust Him. Wait patiently upon Him.

When each time of stillness is ended, write down what came. Keep a journal of these times of visitation so that they will not be lost.

Finally, seek godly counsel and ask brothers and sisters in Christ to keep you accountable. The small circle of friends who make up my support group help me to discern the difference between a real sense of leading from God, and what might be merely the inclination of my ego.

The Only Career Path That Leads to Lasting Success

Each of us must follow the example of our Lord. Each of us must state in clear and distinct terms the life mission that will be the basis for our own self-definition. Then, each of us must commit ourselves to live out our individual mission. Each must be able to say in his or her everyday life: "Forgetting what is behind and straining toward what is ahead, I press on toward the goal to win the prize for which God has called me heavenward in Christ Jesus" (Phil. 3:13-14).

*This material was compiled from the following sources:

Campolo, Tony. *Who Switched the Price Tags?* Waco, Tex.: Word, 1987. Used by permission.

Campolo, Tony. *Everything You've Heard Is Wrong.* Waco, Tex.: Word, 1992. Used by permission.

Background Scripture: Isa. 40:31; Phil. 3:13-14; 1 Kings 19:11-12

Tony Campolo is a professor of sociology at Eastern College in St. Davids, Pa.

▼▼▼

A Quick Look Ahead

- We get sick when we want to look strong. We babble something inappropriate when we want to appear wise. We reach for some shining star of personal achievement and trip over ourselves like Bozo the clown. We stumble. All of us.

- We stumble because we have limited bodies. Sometimes we think we're built of titanium steel. It isn't so. The label on humankind lists one ingredient—dust.

- We stumble because we have limited wisdom. We find two or three jigsaw pieces under a couch cushion and think we have the big picture. We don't.

- We stumble because we have limited faith. Jesus said that if we had faith the size of a mustard seed, we could be chucking elm trees into Lake Erie or rearranging the Rockies. Or something to that effect.

- Every time the Bible gives us a peek at the daunting prospect of our human limitations, it immediately hurls us over the fence into the sufficiency of Jesus Christ.

118

13

We're Only Human, but God Loves Us Anyhow

by Larry Libby

HE LONGED for a single dazzling moment. A defining performance in a long and storied career.

It was a state dinner in Tokyo. The political and economic shoguns* of Japan arranged themselves around a table that shone with white silk, gold utensils, and brilliant floral arrangements. American business moguls were there, too, silently willing their leader to throw all the condescending smiles back in their hosts' faces. The world's media packed the back of the hall, microphones open, videocameras rolling.

Trouble was, he'd been feeling a little funny all morning. A little light-headed. A little shaky. But this was one of those times when personal comfort had to be shunted aside. These meetings—this very dinner—carried huge implications for American business and the world economy. He simply had to be in top form. He simply had to make a commanding impression.

He had just worked his way through the second course—raw salmon with caviar—and was now staring dubiously at the third—grilled beef with pepper sauce. He turned to his left and nodded at his smiling host.

Then he threw up in the prime minister's lap and tumbled to the floor.

As his alarmed wife, security agents, and personal physician knelt on the floor beside him, he groaned, "Roll me under the table until the dinner's over."

Lying there on that fine, oriental carpet, President George Bush may have been thinking about the videotape. He may have been visualizing CNN replaying the whole thing. Over and over. In prime time. In slow motion. In full color.

A little later, when the press secretary stood before the massed media of the Western world, he was obliged to say what ought to have been obvious to everyone.

"The president," he said, "is a human being. The president gets the flu like everyone else."

If he'd been on his toes that morning, the press secretary might have reached back a couple of millennia for a quote that says it all. In all the succeeding centuries, no one has said it more succinctly than the apostle James: "We all stumble in many ways" (3:2).

We get sick when we want to look strong. We babble something inappropriate when we want to appear wise. We reach for some shining star of personal achievement and trip over ourselves like Bozo the clown.

We stumble. All of us. And we do it in 10,000 ways.

Consider young Miss Mott, meeting her boyfriend's parents for the first time. They had gone to an elegant restaurant. Everyone felt a little stiff trying to make conversation.

Then events took an unfortunate turn. The humiliated young woman's letter to her mother was reprinted in the pages of *Campus Life:*

> I did everything you taught me, Mom. I coordi-

nated my clothing the night before, wore clean under-wear, brushed my teeth, arrived promptly, sat up straight, kept my elbows off the table, smiled, listened attentively to the conversation and contributed to it intelligently. You would have been proud.

When my Tab with a lemon twist arrived, I raised my glass to my lips—ramming the plastic straw up my right nostril. Blood squirted from my nose and dripped onto the white silk blouse you gave me for my birthday. I wanted to die! I didn't know what to do first: cry, call you, or pull out the straw, which was still stuck in my nose and pointing directly at Scott's mom's raised eyebrow!

Why is it that our most horrific gaffes occur when we most want to make a favorable impression? Like the time I was an editor at Multnomah Press, visiting our most prominent author, Charles Swindoll.

My associate and I were seated in his office, laboring to make our best pitch for a new book. I wore a new pin-striped business suit, like the slick guys from the big publishing houses, but I was still nervous.

My colleague was executing her role splendidly, explaining our company's reputation for dignity and quality workmanship. Suddenly, she glanced over at me, and her eyes grew round as silver dollars. Then she burst out laughing and pointed at my face. Chuck turned in his chair and then he, too, threw back his head and let loose his trademark laugh.

I had been listening so intently to the interchange that I didn't notice I'd been sucking on the business end of a ballpoint pen. My lips and one front tooth were smeared midnight blue.

I know all about stumbling. So do you. And it isn't always cute or funny. We can hurt ourselves in those humili-

ating pratfalls. Worse still, we can hurt others. It's embar-
rassing. It's humbling. It's as frustrating as it can be.

Scripture reveals three reasons for our stumbling. Understanding those reasons won't eliminate the problem,
but it will help us look at it through God's eyes.

We Stumble Because We Have Limited Bodies

"As a father has compassion on his children," David
wrote in the Psalms, "so the Lord has compassion on those
who fear him; for he knows how we are formed, he remembers that we are dust" (103:13-14).

He remembers, but we forget. Sometimes we think
we're built of titanium steel. It isn't so. The label on humankind lists one ingredient—dust.

There's only so much strength in these arms. There are
only so many miles in these legs. There are only so many
tears in these eyes. I can't do everything I want to do; I can't
do everything I should do. I can't live up to all my expectations for myself, let alone all of others' expectations for me.

When Paul speaks of the piercingly bright and beautiful life of Christ within us, he reminds us that "we have
this treasure in jars of clay to show that this all-surpassing
power is from God and not from us" (2 Cor. 4:7).

I'm not the treasure. I'm only a clay pot that happens
to contain the treasure. I'm a cardboard shoe box stuffed
with thousand-dollar bills, a rusty can enclosing the Hope
diamond. Yes, I was fearfully and wonderfully made, but
in the final analysis, I'm only 161 pounds of intricately
crafted potting soil.

Scripture says God remembers that. He takes it into
account. It's a fact He keeps in mind as He muses over our
life's journey. We should too.

"Watch and pray," Jesus warned His men. "The spirit
is willing, but the body is weak" (Matt. 26:41).

We Stumble Because We Have Limited Wisdom

When the apostle Paul said, "We know in part" (1 Cor. 13:9), he was being kind. Sometimes we don't know much at all. We find two or three jigsaw pieces under a couch cushion and think we have the big picture. We don't. For all our good intentions, our lack of perspective and understanding often causes us to stumble badly.

My heart went out to the young father in Portland, Oreg., who was playing with his one-year-old boy in the family's backyard. The heat had been so severe that summer day, he decided to gently spray his toddler with the garden hose. It never occurred to him that the water in the hose, after sitting all day in the sun, would be scalding.

The baby was hospitalized with burns over 75 percent of his body. This young dad sat in the hospital waiting room, enduring the stares and frowns of emergency room personnel, wondering where in the world he had become separated from his brain.

It's a wonder that children ever survive rookie parents. I can remember trying to treat my son's severe diaper rash with rubbing alcohol. *Well,* I reasoned, *it's clean, it's cool, it's sanitary.* It was also about the most painful thing I could have inflicted on my little guy. I knew it in an instant and felt like a terminal idiot.

It wasn't sinful. It wasn't malicious. It was just garden-variety stupid.

A young Bible school student came to my office some time ago with a piece of writing he was especially proud of. He said, "Give me a critique. Tear this thing apart. Scribble all over it with red ink. Be brutal."

That's what he said. What he meant was, "I really respect you and long for your affirmation. I've just poured my heart and my fragile self-esteem into these three sheets of onionskin paper. A lot of other things have been going wrong in my life, and it would mean the world to me to hear a little encouragement."

For some reason I chose to listen to his words rather than the all-too-obvious plea of his heart. I tore into his article like a kid pounding a piñata. He left my office deeply hurt, and to my knowledge, never tried creative writing again.

What a bungled opportunity! But I will do things like that. We all will. We will hurt people by what we say, and we'll hurt them by what we don't say. We will wound our loved ones through what we do, and we'll bruise them even worse through what we fail to do. We are limited in wisdom. "My people are destroyed from lack of knowledge," the Lord told the prophet (Hos. 4:6). Scripture tells us that again and again. We just have trouble believing it.

We Stumble Because We Have Limited Faith

Jesus said that if we had faith the size of a mustard seed, we could be chucking elm trees into Lake Erie or rearranging the Rockies. Or something to that effect. (See Matt. 17:20.)

If that's what a tiny seed's worth can do, I guess my faith wouldn't show up with an electron microscope. I've seen God's power and grace and sovereignty again and again. I've seen Him crack hearts of granite, move events and circumstances like Monopoly tokens, chase hell out of dark corners, and pull me out of pits so deep that the light at the top looked like a low-wattage firefly.

I've seen all that. But do I believe He can help me through today's set of problems? Like the disciples who worried about their evening snack after watching the Lord feed 5,000 hungry Bible conferees, I have a hard heart and a notoriously short memory.

I'm told that He can do "immeasurably more than all we ask or imagine" (Eph. 3:20). But I ask very little and imagine even less. As a result, I often stumble.

We'll Stumble, but We Need Not Fall

These reminders could be discouraging. But every time the Bible gives us a peek at the daunting prospect of our human limitations, it immediately hurls us over the fence into the sufficiency of Jesus Christ.

David penned, "If the Lord delights in a man's way, he makes his steps firm; though he stumble, he will not fall, for the Lord upholds him with his hand" (Ps. 37:23-24).

Asaph cried out, "My flesh and my heart may fail, but God is the strength of my heart and my portion forever" (Ps. 73:26).

Paul affirmed, "Therefore I will boast all the more gladly about my weaknesses, so that Christ's power may rest on me. . . . For when I am weak, then I am strong" (2 Cor. 12:9-10).

My 11-year-old son and I went for a bike ride last summer through the back roads of central Oregon. I mounted my sleek Japanese road bike; he pedaled his department store mountain bike. His wasn't much of a bike, but he'd saved paper route earnings for months and bought it proudly with his own money.

We had dreamed of this ride through a long, wet Portland winter. And now that we were finally out in the sun together, I almost ruined it.

He was going so *slow*. I wanted to fly down those country roads. And then his shifters weren't working right. Every time he tried to downshift or upshift, he slowed to a crawl and his derailleur rattled like a tommy gun.

I got impatient with him. I berated him for his slowness. I said he could do a lot better if he tried and that it was spoiling our bike ride.

He wept.

He was trying his best, he said, but his new bike just wasn't working very well. We stopped together out in the pine trees and sunshine, and I watched him . . . head bowed, tears rolling down his cheeks.

I felt like a wretch. I embraced him and told him I was sorry for my foolish impatience.

Now if my heart was moved, human as I am, by my son's limitations, how does my Heavenly Father feel when I can't keep up and my gears get jammed and my legs get tired? What does He think about me when my dreams fall short? And I've pushed myself to my limits? And I stop by the side of the road to weep in frustration and sorrow?

Does He stay on His bike and say, "Too bad, kid. Your legs are too short to bike with God"? No. Unlike us humans, God doesn't yell at me out of ignorance first.

Instead, He climbs off, puts His arms around me, and says, "I'll never leave you behind, Son. It doesn't really matter how far we go, because being with you on this ride is what really matters."

We all stumble in many ways. We waste our opportunities, miss our cues, ram straws up our nostrils, reach higher than we can grasp, and sometimes even throw up on the prime minister's lap.

Ultimately, we fail because we are fallible. God knows all about that—and loves us through it all. He has a long track record of working with stumbling, fumbling, ham-handed, weak-stomached servants like you and me.

But we'll never finish the job unless we crawl out from under the table.

*Businessmen of exceptional wealth, power, and influence.

Background Scripture: Pss. 37:23-24; 73:26; 2 Cor. 4:7

Larry Libby is senior editor for Questar Publishers in Sisters, Oreg.